American Red Cross

COMMUNITY
CPR

✚ American Red Cross

COMMUNITY
CPR

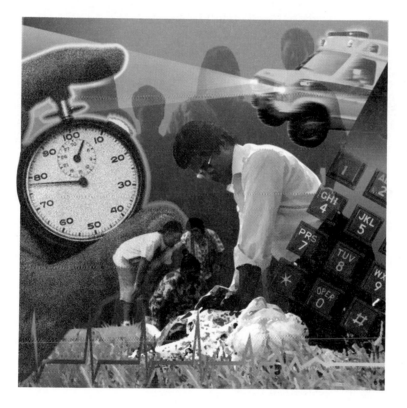

Mosby
Lifeline

St. Louis Baltimore Boston Chicago London Philadelphia Sydney Toronto

This participant's textbook is an integral part of
American Red Cross training. By itself, it does not constitute complete
and comprehensive training.

The emergency care procedures outlined in this book reflect the
standard of knowledge and accepted emergency practices in the
United States at the time this book was published. It is the reader's
responsibility to stay informed of changes in the emergency
care procedures.

Printed in the United States of America.

Mosby Lifeline
Mosby–Year Book, Inc.
11830 Westline Industrial Drive
St. Louis, MO 63146

Library of Congress Cataloging in Publication Data

Community CPR / American Red Cross.
    p.   cm.
  Includes index.
  ISBN 0-8016-7066-7
  1. CPR (First aid)   I. American Red Cross.   II. Mosby-Year Book.
RC87.9.C65 1993   92-584
616.02′52—dc20   CIP

93 94 95 96 97 CL/CD/BA 9 8 7 6 5 4 3 2

ACKNOWLEDGEMENTS

This course and participant's manual were developed and produced through a joint effort of the American Red Cross and the Mosby–Year Book Publishing Company. Many individuals shared in the overall process in supportive, technical, and creative ways. This manual could not have been developed without the dedication of both paid and volunteer staff. Their commitment to excellence made this manual possible.

The Health and Safety Program Development staff at American Red Cross national headquarters responsible for the instructional design and writing of this course and manual included: Lawrence D. Newell, Ed.D., NREMT-P, Project Manager; Martha F. Beshers; Thomas J.S. Edwards, Ph.D.; M. Elizabeth Buoy-Morrissey, M.P.H.; Robert T. Ogle; and S. Elizabeth White, M.A.Ed., ATC, Associates; Sandra D. Buesking, Lori M. Compton, Marian F.H. Kirk, and O. Paul Stearns, Analysts. Administrative support was provided by Denise Beale and Ella Holloway.

The following American Red Cross national headquarters Health and Safety volunteer and paid staff provided guidance and review: Robert F. Burnside, Director; Frank Carroll, Manager, Program Development; Richard M. Walter, Manager, Operations; and Stephen Silverman, Ed.D., National Volunteer Consultant for Program Development.

The Mosby Lifeline publishing team based in Hanover, Maryland included: David Culverwell, Vice President and Publisher; Claire Merrick, Senior Editor; Richard Weimer, Executive Editor; and Dana Battaglia, Assistant Editor.

The Mosby–Year Book Editorial and Production Team based in St. Louis, Missouri, included: Virgil Mette, Executive Vice President; Carol Sullivan Wiseman, Project Manager; Diana Lyn Laulainen, Production Editor; Kay Kramer, Director of Art and Design; Jerry A. Wood, Director of Manufacturing; Patricia Stinecipher, Special Product Manager; and Kathy Grone, Manufacturing Supervisor.

Special thanks go to Rick Brady, Photographer and Kathy Barkey, Designer.

Guidance and review were also provided by the members of the American Red Cross CPR/First Aid Advisory Group including:

Ray Cranston
Chairperson
Commanding Officer, Traffic Safety Unit
Farmington Hills Police Department
Farmington Hills, Michigan

Larry Bair
Director, Health and Safety and Tissue Services
Central Iowa Chapter
Des Moines, Iowa

John E. Hendrickson
Director, Safety and Health
Mid-America Chapter
Chicago, Illinois

Andra Jones
Director, Health and Safety
Central Mississippi Chapter
Jackson, Mississippi

Sherri Olson-Roberts
Director, Health and Safety
Washtenaw County Chapter
Ann Arbor, Michigan

James A. Otte
Chairman, Health and Safety Committee
Glynn County Chapter
Brunswick, Georgia

Teresita B. Ramirez
Centex County Chapter
Lecturer, Department of Curriculum and Instruction
The University of Texas at Austin
Austin, Texas

W. Douglas Round
Captain, Greeley Fire Department
Colorado Territory
Greeley, Colorado

Natalie Lynne Smith, M.S.
Greater Hartford Chapter
Farmington, Connecticut

Linda S. Wenger
Director, Health and Safety
Lancaster County Chapter
Lancaster, Pennsylvania

David J. Wurzer, Ph.D.
Greater Long Beach Chapter
Long Beach, California

External review was provided by the following organizations and individuals:

Gloria M. Blatti, RN, FNP, EdD
Adelphi University
Long Island, New York

Nisha C. Chandra, MD
Division of Cardiology
Francis Scott Key Medical Center
Baltimore, Maryland

Loring S. Flint, MD
Vice President
Baystate Medical Center
Springfield, Massachusetts

Robert C. Luten, MD
Director, Pediatric EMS
University of Florida
Health Science Center—Jacksonville
Jacksonville, Florida

John A. Paraskos, MD
Associate Director of C.V. Medicine
University of Massachusetts, Medical School
Worcester, Massachusetts

James S. Seidel, MD, PhD
Associate Professor of UCLA
Chief, Ambulatory Pediatrics
Torrance, California

Jay Shaw
Associate Professor
Eastern Montana College
American Red Cross Midland Empire Chapter
Board of Directors, Supervisory Committee
Billings, Montana

Edward Stapleton, EMT-P
Department of Emergency Medicine
Health Sciences Center
State University of New York at Stoney Brook
Stoney Brook, New York

ABOUT THIS COURSE

People need to know what to do in an emergency before medical help arrives. Since you may be faced with an emergency in your lifetime, it's important that you know how to recognize an emergency and how to respond. The intent of this course is to help people feel more confident of their ability to act appropriately in the event of an emergency.

After you complete this course, we believe you will be able to—
• Identify ways to prevent injury and/or illness.
• Recognize when an emergency has occurred.
• Follow three emergency action steps in any emergency.
• Provide basic care for injury and/or sudden illness until the victim can receive professional medical help.

To help you achieve this goal, you will read information in this manual, view a series of video segments, and participate in a number of learning activities designed to increase your knowledge and skills.

In addition, this course emphasizes the value of a safe and healthy life-style. It attempts to alert you to behavior and situations that contribute to your risk of injury and/or illness and to motivate you to take precautions and make any necessary life-style changes.

This manual contains all the material you learn in class in a form you can keep and refer to whenever you wish. Highlighted information and material condensed in lists make it easy for you to identify the critical points and to refresh your memory quickly. Photos, drawings, graphs, and tables also present information in an easy-to-find form. Skill sheets give step-by-step directions for performing the skills taught in the course. Questionnaires provide a way for you to evaluate certain risks in your life-style. Articles of varying lengths cover all the topics taught. Features contain information that enhances the information in the articles.

You may be taking this course not only because you feel a need to learn what to do if faced with an emergency but because of a job requirement specifying that you complete training and achieve a specific level of competency on both skill and written evaluations. In this case the American Red Cross provides a certification card. You will be eligible to receive a certificate if you—
• Perform specific skills competently and demonstrate the ability to make appropriate decisions for care.
• Pass a final written exam with a score of 80 percent or higher.

If you do not have a job requirement to achieve a specific level of competency on both skill and written evaluations, you will not need a certification card. You will also not need to take the final examination. You will be acknowledged for your attendance and participation.

HEALTH PRECAUTIONS AND GUIDELINES DURING TRAINING

The American Red Cross has trained millions of people in first aid and CPR (cardiopulmonary resuscitation), using manikins as training aids. According to the Centers for Disease Control (CDC), there has never been a documented case of any disease caused by bacteria, a fungus, or a virus transmitted through the use of training aids, such as manikins used for CPR.

The Red Cross follows widely accepted guidelines for cleaning and decontaminating training manikins. **If these guidelines are adhered to, the risk of any kind of disease transmission during training is extremely low.**

To help minimize the risk of disease transmission, you should follow some basic health precautions and guidelines while participating in training. You should take precautions if you have a condition that would increase your risk or other participants' risk of exposure to infections. Request a separate training manikin if you—

- Have an acute condition, such as a cold, a sore throat, or cuts or sores on your hands or around your mouth.
- Know you are seropositive (have had a positive blood test) for hepatitis B surface antigen (HBsAg), indicating that you are currently infected with the hepatitis B virus.*
- Know you have a chronic infection indicated by long-term seropositivity (long-term positive blood tests) for hepatitis B surface antigen (HBsAg)* or a positive blood test for anti–HIV (that is, a positive test for antibodies to HIV, the virus that causes many severe infections including AIDS).
- Have a type of condition that makes you unusually likely to get an infection.

*A person with hepatitis B infection will test positive for the hepatitis B surface antigen (HBsAg). Most persons infected with hepatitis B will get better within a period of time. However, some hepatitis B infections will become chronic and linger for much longer. These persons will continue to test positive for HBsAg. Their decision to participate in CPR training should be guided by their physician.
After a person has had an acute hepatitis B infection, he or she will no longer test positive for the surface antigen but will test positive for the hepatitis B antibody (anti-HBs). Persons who have been vaccinated for hepatitis B will also test positive for the hepatitis B antibody. A positive test for the hepatitis B antibody (anti-HBs) should not be confused with a positive test for the hepatitis B surface antigen (HBsAg).

If you decide you should have your own manikin, ask your instructor if he or she can provide one for you to use. You will not be asked to explain why in your request. The manikin will not be used by anyone else until it has been cleaned according to the recommended end-of-class decontamination procedures. The number of manikins available for class use is limited. Therefore the more advance notice you give, the more likely it is that you can be provided a separate manikin.

In addition to taking the precautions regarding manikins, you can further protect yourself and other participants from infection by following these guidelines:

- Wash your hands thoroughly before participating in class activities.
- Do not eat, drink, use tobacco products, or chew gum during classes when manikins are used.
- Clean the manikin properly before use. For some manikins, this means vigorously wiping the manikin's face and the inside of its mouth with a clean gauze pad soaked with either a solution of liquid chlorine bleach and water (sodium hypochlorite and water) or rubbing alcohol. For other manikins, it means changing the rubber face. Your instructor will provide you with instructions for cleaning the type of manikin used in your class.
- Follow the guidelines provided by your instructor when practicing skills such as clearing a blocked airway with your finger.

Training in first aid and CPR requires physical activity. If you have a medical condition or disability that will prevent you from taking part in the practice sessions, please let your instructor know.

CONTENTS

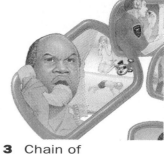

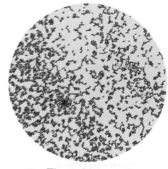

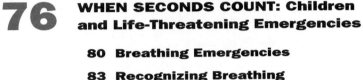

SKILL SHEETS

American Red Cross

COMMUNITY
CPR

Why did you say you'd get to the party by seven o'clock? It's a good thing you stopped at the convenience store now and not later. Only a couple of things to buy. Why are all those people standing around over there? Oh no! It's the person who works here. . . . You leave the car and see the young man lying on his back, looking dazed, and holding his head. Even though a crowd has gathered, no one is helping him. They are just looking at each other. He needs help from some-one. That someone could be you!

If not YOU... Who?

GET INVOLVED

If placed in the above situation, would you step forward to help? "I hope I never have to," is what you are probably saying to yourself. However, given the number of injuries and sudden illnesses that occur in the United States each year, you might well have to deal with an emergency situation someday.

Consider the following:

• About 2 million people are hospitalized each year because of injuries, and injuries result in nearly 142,500 deaths each year.

- Infectious diseases used to cause the greatest concern about the health of children, but now, unintentional injuries cause most childhood deaths. Injuries also cause millions of heart-stopping moments each year. In fact, injuries are the leading cause of death and disability in children and young adults.

- More than 6 million people in the United States have cardiovascular disease. Cardiovascular disease causes about 1 million deaths in the United States each year. That's nearly half of the deaths that occur each year!

- Over 500,000 Americans have strokes each year, and 150,000 Americans die each year from stroke.

Each time a person is injured or experiences a sudden illness, such as a heart attack or a stroke, someone has to do something to help. You may find yourself in the position of having to provide help someday.

Everyone should know what to do in an emergency. You should know who to call and what care to provide. Providing care involves giving first aid until professional medical help arrives. Everyone should know first aid, but even if you haven't had any first aid training, you can still help in an emergency.

Calling your local emergency phone number is the most important thing you can do. The sooner medical help arrives, the better a person's chances of surviving a life-threatening emergency. You play a

Everyone Should Know What to Do in an Emergency ...

Everyone Should Know First Aid.

major role in making the emergency medical services (EMS) system work effectively. The EMS system is a network of police, fire, and medical personnel, as well as other community resources.

Your role in the EMS system includes four basic steps:
1. *Recognize* that an emergency exists.
2. *Decide* to act.
3. *Call* the local emergency telephone number for help.
4. *Provide* care until help arrives.

Of course, steps 3 and 4 won't happen if you don't take steps 1 and 2. By recognizing an emergency and taking action to help,

Leading Causes of Death
ages 0 to 44

Accidents 53,027

Cancer 24,675

Heart Disease 22,327

Homicide 18,577

Suicide 17,006

Monthly Vital Statistics. Vol. 40, No. 8, Supplement 2. Jan. 7, 1992.

1. Citizen Response

2. Calling the Emergency Number

3. First Responder Care

4. EMT Care

5. Hospital Care

6. Rehabilitation

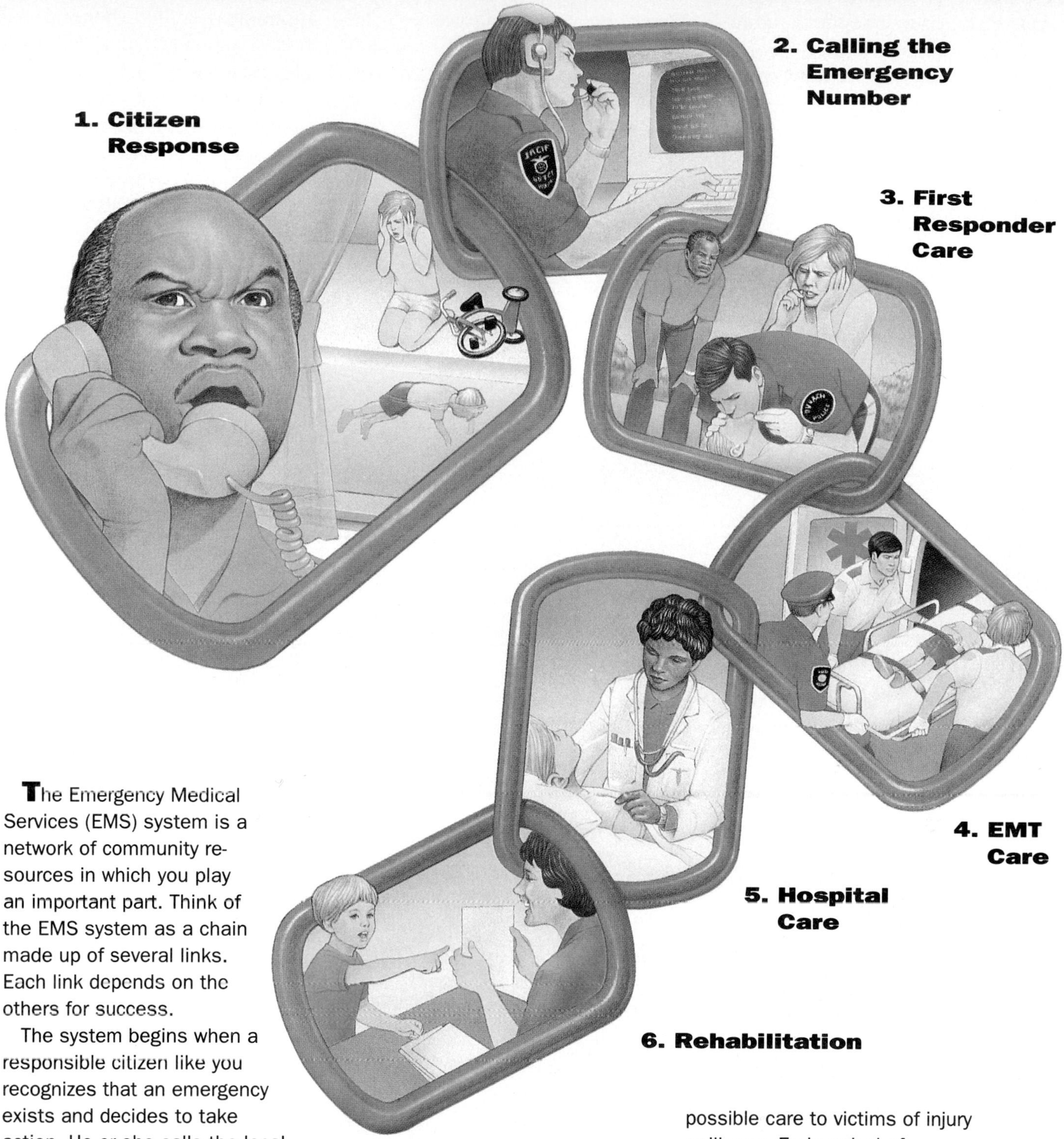

The Emergency Medical Services (EMS) system is a network of community resources in which you play an important part. Think of the EMS system as a chain made up of several links. Each link depends on the others for success.

The system begins when a responsible citizen like you recognizes that an emergency exists and decides to take action. He or she calls the local emergency number for help. The EMS dispatcher answers the call and uses the information you give to determine what help is needed. A team of emergency personnel give care at the scene and transport the victim to the hospital where emergency department staff and a variety of other professionals take over.

Ideally, a victim will move through each link in the chain. All the links should work together to provide the best possible care to victims of injury or illness. Early arrival of emergency personnel increases the victim's chances of surviving a life-threatening emergency. Whether or not you know first aid, calling your emergency number is the most important action you can take.

you give injured or ill persons the best chance for survival. Know your local emergency telephone number. The rapid arrival of professional help increases the victim's chances of surviving a life-threatening emergency.

RECOGNIZING EMERGENCIES

Emergencies can happen to anyone and they can happen anywhere, but before you can give help you must be able to recognize an emergency. You may realize that an emergency has occurred only if something unusual attracts your attention. For example, you may become aware of unusual noises, sights, odors, and appearances or behaviors.

Noises that may signal an emergency include screaming or calls for help; breaking glass, crashing metal, or screeching tires; a change in the sound made by machinery or equipment; or sudden, loud noises, like those made by collapsing buildings or falling ladders or when a person falls.

Signals of an emergency that you may see include a person lying motionless, spilled chemicals, fallen boxes, a power failure or downed electrical wires, or smoke or fire.

Many odors are part of our everyday lives, for example, gasoline fumes at a gas station, the smell of chlorine at a swimming pool, and the smell of chemicals at a refinery. However, when these are stronger than usual, there may be an emergency. Also, an unusual odor may mean something is wrong. Put your own safety first. Leave the area if there is an unusual or very strong odor, since some fumes are poisonous.

It may be difficult to tell if someone is behaving strangely or if something is wrong, especially if you don't know the person. Some actions leave little doubt that something might be wrong. For example, if you see someone suddenly collapse or slip and fall, you have a fairly good idea that the person might need some help.

Other signals of a possible emergency might not be as easy to recognize. They include signals of breathing difficulty, confused behavior, unusual skin color, signs of pain or discomfort, such as clutching the chest or throat or being doubled over, or facial expressions indicating something is wrong.

Sometimes it is obvious that something is wrong; at other times it is more difficult to be sure. For example, a person having a heart attack may clutch his or her chest, begin to perspire, and have difficulty breathing. Another heart attack victim may only feel mild chest pain and not give any obvious signals of distress. The important thing is to recognize that an emergency might have occurred.

RECOGNIZING EMERGENCIES

Your senses—hearing, sight, and smell—may help you recognize an emergency. Emergencies are often signaled by something unusual that catches your attention.

UNUSUAL NOISES
Screams, yells, moans, or calls for help
Breaking glass, crashing metal, or screeching tires
Changes in machinery or equipment noises
Sudden, loud voices

UNUSUAL SIGHTS
A stalled vehicle
An overturned pot
A spilled medicine container
Broken glass
Downed electrical wires
Smoke or fire

UNUSUAL ODORS
Odors that are stronger than usual
Unrecognizable odors

UNUSUAL APPEARANCES OR BEHAVIORS
Difficulty breathing
Clutching the chest or throat
Slurred, confused, or hesitant speech
Unexplainable confusion or drowsiness
Sweating for no apparent reason
Unusual skin color

DECIDING TO ACT

Once you recognize an emergency has occurred, you must decide whether to help and how you can best help. There are many ways you can help in an emergency. *In order to help, you must act.*

▼

There are Many Ways to Help in an Emergency. In Order to Help, You Must Act.

Whether or not you have had first aid training, being faced with an emergency will probably cause you to have mixed feelings. Besides wanting to help, you may have other feelings that make you hesitate or back away from the situation. These feelings are personal and very real. The decision to act is yours and yours alone.

Sometimes, even though people recognize that what has happened is an emergency, they fail to act. There are many reasons why people don't act in an emergency. The most common factors that influence a person's response include—

• The presence of other people.
• Uncertainty about the victim.
• The type of injury or illness.

What Everyone Should Know About Good Samaritan Laws

Are there laws to protect you when you help in an emergency situation?

Yes, most states have enacted Good Samaritan laws. These laws give legal protection to people who provide emergency care to ill or injured persons.

When citizens respond to an emergency and act as a *reasonable* and *prudent* person would under the same conditions, Good Samaritan immunity generally prevails. This legal immunity protects you, as a rescuer, from being sued and found financially responsible for the victim's injury. For example, a reasonable and prudent person would—

■ Move a victim only if the victim's life was endangered.
■ Ask a conscious victim for permission before giving care.
■ Check the victim for life-threatening emergencies before providing further care.
■ Summon professional help to the scene by calling the local emergency number or the operator.
■ Continue to provide care until more highly trained personnel arrive.

Good Samaritan laws were developed to encourage people to help others in emergency situations. They require that the "Good Samaritan" use common sense and a reasonable level of skill, not to exceed the scope of the individual's training in emergency situations. They assume each person would do his or her best to save a life or prevent further injury.

People are rarely sued for helping in an emergency. However, the existence of Good Samaritan laws does not mean that someone cannot sue. In rare cases, courts have ruled that these laws do not apply in cases when an individual rescuer's response was grossly or willfully negligent or reckless or when the rescuer abandoned the victim after initiating care.

If you are interested in finding out your state's Good Samaritan laws, contact a legal professional or check with your local library.

- Fear of catching a disease.
- Fear of doing something wrong.

If there are several people standing around, it might not be easy to tell if anyone is providing first aid. Always ask if you can help. Just because there is a crowd doesn't mean someone is caring for the victim. In fact, you may be the only one there who knows first aid.

Although you may feel embarrassed about coming forward in front of other people, this should not stop you from offering help. Someone has to take action in an emergency, and it may have to be you, even though you don't want to become the center of attention. If others are already giving care, ask if you can help.

If there are people around, but they do not appear to be helping, tell them how to help. You can ask them to call the emergency number, meet the ambulance and direct it to your location, keep the area free of onlookers and traffic, or help give care. You might send them for blankets or other supplies.

Most emergencies happen in or near the home, so you are more likely to give care to a family member or a friend than to someone you do not know. However, this isn't always the case. There may be a time when you do not know the victim and feel uneasy about helping a stranger. Sometimes you might not be sure about taking ac-

FIRST AID

Bacteria and viruses are common forms of germs.

Streptococcus agalactia bacteria

You are driving home from work. Suddenly, you hear a crash. A person on a bike has been hit by a car and is bleeding. You want to help but are afraid. You ask yourself, "Will I catch a disease if I give first aid? How do diseases pass from one person to another? What can I do to protect myself from infection?"

& DISEASE TRANSMISSION

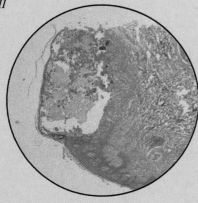

Herpes simplex II virus

It is natural to have questions when helping in an emergency. Therefore it is important to know how diseases are transmitted and how to protect yourself when giving first aid.

Diseases that can pass from one person to another are called infectious diseases. Infectious diseases develop when germs invade the body and cause illness. The most common germs are bacteria and viruses.

Bacteria can live outside the body and do not depend on other organisms for life. The number of bacteria that infect humans is really very small. Some cause serious infections. These can be treated with special medications called antibiotics.

There are Some Simple Things You Can do to Prevent Disease Transmission.

TAKE PRECAUTIONS

Viruses depend on other organisms to live. Once in the body, they are hard to remove. Few medications can fight viruses. The body's immune system is the number one protection against infection.

You may wonder how bacteria and viruses pass from one person to another. Well, in situations that require first aid care, diseases can be transmitted by touching, breathing, and biting.

You can become infected if you touch an infected person, if germs in that person's blood or other body fluids pass into your body through breaks or cuts in the skin or through the lining of your eyes, nose, and mouth. Therefore the greatest risk of infection occurs when you touch blood or other body fluids directly.

You can also be infected when you touch an object that has been soiled by a person's blood or body fluids. Be careful when handling soiled objects. Sharp objects can cut your skin and pass germs. Avoid touching blood and soiled objects with your bare hands.

Some diseases, such as the common cold, are transmitted by the air we breathe. It is possible to become infected if you breathe air exhaled by an infected person. Airborne infection can occur during sneezing, coughing, etc. Most of us are exposed to germs everyday in our jobs, on the bus, or in a crowded restaurant. Fortunately, simply being exposed to these germs is usually not adequate for diseases to be transmitted.

Animals can pass diseases through bites. For example, infected dogs, cats, cattle, and some wild animals can transmit rabies. A human bite also can pass disease. Contracting a disease from a bite is rare in any situation and very uncommon when giving first aid. In an emergency situation, it is unlikely that you will be bitten.

Some diseases are passed more easily than others. We all know how quickly the flu can pass from person to person at home or at work. Although these diseases can create discomfort, they are often temporary and are not serious to healthy adults.

Other diseases can be more serious, such as hepatitis B (HBV) and HIV, which causes AIDS. Although very serious, they are not easily transmitted and are not passed by casual contact, such as shaking hands. The primary way to transmit HBV or HIV is through blood-to-blood contact. By following some basic guidelines, you can help reduce disease transmission when providing first aid:

- Avoid contact with body fluids when possible.
- Place barriers, such as disposable gloves or a clean dry cloth, between the victim's body fluids and yourself.
- Wear protective clothing, such as disposable gloves, to cover any cuts, scrapes, and skin conditions you may have.
- Wash your hands with soap and water immediately after giving care.
- Do not eat, drink, or touch your mouth, nose, or eyes when giving first aid.
- Do not touch objects that may be soiled with blood.
- Be prepared by having a first aid kit handy.

Following these guidelines decreases your risk of getting or transmitting an infectious disease. Remember always to give first aid in ways that protect you and the victim from disease transmission.

You Are More Likely to Give Care to a Family Member or a Friend Than to Someone You do Not Know.

tion because of who the victim is. For example, the victim may be much older or much younger than you, be a different gender or race, have a disabling condition, be of a different status at work, or be a victim of crime.

Sometimes people who have been injured or become suddenly ill act strangely or may be hard to deal with. The injury or illness, stress, or other factors such as the effects of drugs, alcohol, or medications may make people unpleasant or angry. Do not take this behavior personally. If you feel at all threatened by the victim's behavior, leave the immediate area and call your local emergency number for help.

Another factor that affects a person's decision to do something in an emergency is the type of injury or illness. An injury or illness may sometimes be very unpleasant. Blood, vomit, unpleasant odors, and deformed body parts or torn or burned skin upset almost everyone. You may have to turn away for a

moment and take a few deep breaths to get control of your feelings. Then try to provide care. If you still cannot give first aid because of the way the injury looks, you can ensure your safety and the safety of victims and bystanders, and you can make sure you or someone has called the local emergency number.

Disease transmission in a first aid situation is another issue that concerns many people. Nowadays, people worry about the possibility of catching a disease while giving first aid. This is especially true as a result of the AIDS epidemic. This concern is understandable. However, the actual risk of catching a disease when giving first aid is far less than you may think.

Giving first aid does not mean that you will automatically catch a disease. In fact, it is extremely unlikely that you will catch a disease by giving first aid. If you do not have any cuts or sores, your skin protects you as you give first aid. Remember that disease transmis-

sion works both ways. You can also pass diseases to the victim if you have any cuts or sores on your own skin.

Emergency situations that involve contact with body fluids, such as bleeding, have the possibility of transmitting disease. There are simple things you can do to minimize the chance of infection. Always take precautions to prevent direct contact with a victim's body fluids while you are giving first aid. When they are available, use protective barriers, such as disposable gloves or a clean cloth, to stop bleeding. The victim may even be able to use his or her own hand to help. Afterward, wash thoroughly as soon as possible, even if you wore gloves. Tell your doctor if you come in direct contact with a victim's body fluids while giving first aid.

Remember that you are most likely to use your first aid skills to help someone you know personally, such as a family member, friend, or co-worker. In some instances, you may know this person's health status and be aware of the risk of infection.

People react differently in emergencies. Whether trained in first aid or not, some people are afraid of doing the wrong thing and making matters worse. If you are not sure what to do, call your local emergency number for professional help. *The worst thing to do is nothing.*

Sometimes people worry that they might be sued for giving first aid. In fact, lawsuits against people who give emergency care at a scene of an accident are highly unusual and rarely successful. Most states have enacted "Good Samaritan" laws. These laws protect people who willingly give first aid without accepting anything in return. So you can help without worrying about lawsuits.

FACTS ABOUT AIDS

Human Immunodeficiency Virus

The Disease: AIDS stands for acquired immune deficiency syndrome. It is caused by the human immunodeficiency virus (HIV). When the virus gets into the body, it damages the immune system, the body system that fights infection. Once the virus enters the body, it can grow quietly in the body for months or even years. People infected with HIV might not feel or appear sick. Eventually, the weakened immune system gives way to certain types of infections.

How the Disease is Transmitted: The virus enters the body in three basic ways:
- Through direct contact with the bloodstream. *Example:* Sharing an unsterilized needle with an HIV-positive person to inject drugs into the veins.
- Through the mucous membranes lining the eyes, mouth, throat, rectum, and vagina. *Example:* Having unprotected sex with an HIV-positive person—male or female.
- Through the womb, birth canal, or breast milk. *Example:* Being infected as an unborn child or shortly after birth by an infected mother.

The virus cannot enter through the skin unless there is a cut or break in the skin. Even then, the possibility of infection is very low unless there is direct contact for a lengthy period of time. Saliva is not known to transmit HIV.

Prevention: Your behavior can put you at risk for getting AIDS. Using intravenous drugs, especially with unsterilized needles, or having sex without protection, such as condoms, are high-risk activities.

First Aid Precautions: The likelihood of HIV transmission during a first aid situation is very low. You are most likely to give first aid to someone you know, such as a family member or close friend. Always give care in ways that protect you and the victim from disease transmission. If possible, wash your hands before and after giving care, even if you wear gloves. Avoid touching or being splashed by another person's body fluids, especially blood. Be prepared with a first aid kit that includes waterless antiseptic hand cleaners and disposable gloves.

Testing: If you think you have put yourself at risk, get tested. A blood test will tell whether or not your body is producing antibodies in response to the virus. If you are not sure whether you should be tested, call your doctor, the public health department, or the AIDS hot line listed below and talk to them. In the meantime, don't participate in activities that put anyone else at risk.

Blood Supply: Since 1985, all donated blood in the United States has been tested for HIV. As a result, the blood supply is considered safe. The risk of becoming infected through a blood transfusion is very low.

Hot Line: If you have questions, call the national AIDS hot line at 1-800-342-AIDS, 24 hours a day, 7 days a week, or the SIDA hot line (Spanish) at 1-800-344-SIDA, 8 a.m.-2 a.m., EST, 7 days a week. TTY/TDD service is available at 1-800-243-7TTY, Monday-Friday, 10 a.m.-10 p.m., EST, or call your state health department.

Keep information about you and your family in a handy place, such as on the refrigerator door or in your automobile glove compartment.

▼

Keep medical and insurance records up-to-date.

▼

Find out if your community is served by an emergency 9-1-1 telephone number. If it is not, look up the numbers for the police, fire department, EMS, and poison control center. Emergency numbers are usually listed in the front of the telephone book. Teach everyone in your home how and when to use these numbers.

▼

Keep emergency telephone numbers in a handy place, such as by the telephone or in the first aid kit. Include home and work numbers of family members and friends who can help. Be sure to keep both lists current.

▼

Keep a first aid kit handy in your home, automobile, workplace, and recreation area.

▼

Learn and practice first aid skills.

▼

Make sure your house or apartment number is easy to read. Numerals are easier to read than spelled-out numbers.

▼

Wear a medical alert tag if you have a potentially serious medical condition, such as epilepsy, diabetes, heart disease, or allergies.

Your decision to act in an emergency should be guided by your own values and by your knowledge of the risks that may be present. Your decision to act might not involve giving first aid. However, it should at least involve calling the local emergency number to get medical help.

PREPARING FOR EMERGENCIES

You will never see the emergencies you prevent. However, emergencies can and do happen, regardless of attempts to prevent them.

If you are prepared for unforeseen emergencies, you can help ensure that care begins as soon as possible—for yourself, your family, and your fellow citizens. If you are trained in first aid, you can give help in the first few minutes of an emergency that can save a life. First aid *can* be the difference between life and death. Often it *does* make the difference between complete recovery and permanent disability.

By knowing what to do, you will be better able to manage your fears and overcome barriers to action. The most important things are to recognize that an emergency has occurred and to call the local emergency telephone number. Then give first aid until help arrives.

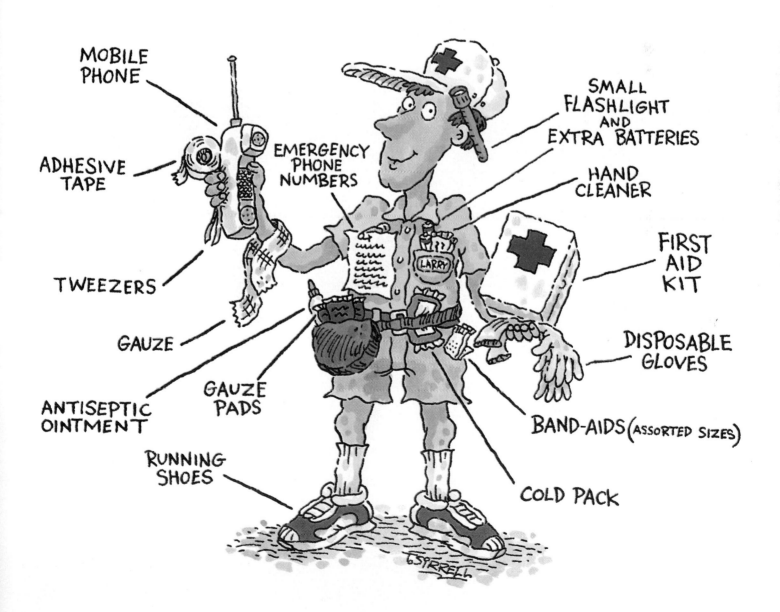

TAKING ACTION

Emergency Action Steps

It's 9:30 on a Saturday morning. The sudden sounds outside are close together but very clear—a screech of brakes, a thud, and a shrill scream. You are out the door and onto the sidewalk before you have time to think about it. Maria and Rose had been playing out there!

People are running from all over. Your eyes take it in — the twisted bike, the van in the middle of the street, and the child lying on the pavement. At least he's alive; he's moaning and crying. His left leg looks funny and there's blood on the pavement. A man is staring at the boy. "He just came out of nowhere," he stammers. "All of a sudden, there he was, right in front of the van." The boy is obviously hurt. What should you do?

So far, you've learned that you can make a difference in an emergency. You may even save a life. You know how to recognize an emergency. You've learned that the worst thing you can do is nothing and deciding to get involved can be hard for anyone—not just you. You also know some things you can do to help.

Even so, when an emergency happens, you may feel confused. However, you can train yourself to stay calm and think before you act. Ask yourself, "What do I need to do? What is the best help I can give?" To answer these questions, you should know three basic steps you can take in any emergency:

1. *Check* the scene and the victim.
2. *Call* 9-1-1 or your local emergency number.
3. *Care* for the victim.

CHECK

Before you can help the victim, you must make sure the scene is safe for you and any bystanders. You also need some information.

Look the scene over and try to answer these questions:

1. Is the scene safe?
2. What happened?
3. How many victims are there?
4. Can bystanders help?

Look for anything that might make the scene unsafe. Examples include spilled chemicals, traffic, fire, escaping steam, downed electrical lines, smoke, extreme weather, and poisonous gas. If these or other dangers threaten, do not go near the victim. Stay at a safe distance and call your local emergency number immediately.

If the scene is still unsafe after you call, stay away from the victim. Don't put yourself in danger. Dead or injured heroes are no help to anyone! Leave dangerous situations to professionals like fire fighters and police who have the training and equipment to deal with them. Once they make the scene safe, you can offer to help.

Try to find out what happened. Look for clues to what caused the emergency and how the victim might be injured. Nearby objects, such as a fallen ladder, broken glass, or a spilled bottle of medicine, may give you information. Your check of the scene may be the only way to tell what happened.

Look carefully for more than one victim. You might not spot everyone at first. If one victim is bleeding or screaming, you might not notice an unconscious victim. It is also easy to overlook a baby or a small child. Once you reach the victim, check the scene again. You may see dangers, clues, or victims you missed before.

Do not move a seriously injured victim unless there is an immediate danger, such as fire, flood, or poisonous gas. If you must move the victim, do it as quickly and carefully as possible. If there is no danger, tell the victim not to move. Tell any bystanders not to move the victim.

You have already learned that the presence of bystanders does not mean that a victim is receiving help. Besides doing what you can for the victim, you can ask bystanders to help. They may be able to tell you what happened or direct you to the nearest telephone. A family member, friend, or co-worker who is present may know if the victim has an illness or a medical condition. The victim may be too upset to answer your questions. A child may be especially frightened. This may also be true for an adult who has been unconscious for a few minutes. Bystanders can also help comfort the victim and others at the scene. Parents or guardians who are present may be able to calm a frightened child. They can also tell you if a child has a medical condition.

When you reach the victim, you must try to find out what is wrong. Look for signals that may indicate a life-threatening emergency. The first thing you check is whether the victim is conscious. Sometimes this is obvious. The victim may be able to speak to you and tell you what happened. The victim may be moaning, crying, or making some other noise. The victim may be moving around. Talk to the victim to reassure him or her and to learn what you can about what happened.

What if the victim is lying on the ground, silent, and not moving? You must find out if the victim is conscious or unconscious. Unconsciousness is a life-threatening emergency. If the victim doesn't respond to you in any way, assume he or she is unconscious. You must call for an ambulance at once!

Look for other signals of injuries that are life-threatening or may become life-threatening: no breathing or breathing with difficulty, no pulse, and/or severe bleeding.

If the victim doesn't respond to you in any way, assume the victim is unconscious. Call for an ambulance at once!

"Do No Further Harm"

One of the most dangerous threats to a seriously injured victim is unnecessary movement. Usually when giving care, you will not face dangers that require you to move a victim. In most cases, you can follow the emergency steps (check, call, and care) where you find the victim. Moving the victim can cause additional injury and pain and complicate the victim's recovery.

There are three general situations in which you should move a victim. The most obvious is when you are faced with immediate danger such as fire, lack of oxygen, risk of explosion, or a collapsing structure.

A second reason to move a victim is if you have to get to another victim who may have a more serious problem. In this case, you may have to move a victim with minor injuries to reach one who needs care immediately. Third, you may have to move the victim to provide proper care. For example, someone who has collapsed and does not have a pulse, needs cardiopulmonary resuscitation (CPR). CPR needs to be performed on a firm, flat surface. If the surface or space is not adequate to provide care, the victim should be moved.

Once you decide to move a victim, you must quickly decide *how* to move the victim. Carefully consider your safety and the safety of the victim. Base your decision on the dangers you are facing, the size and condition of the victim, your ability and condition, and whether you have any help.

You can improve your chances of successfully moving a victim without injuring yourself. When you lift, use your legs, not your back. Bend your body at the knees and hips and avoid twisting your body. Walk forward when possible, taking small steps, and looking where you are going.

Avoid twisting or bending the victim with a possible head or spine injury. Do not move a victim who is too large to move comfortably.

You can help support a victim who is conscious and who can walk with assistance. Place the victim's arm over your shoulders and hold it in place with your hand. Support the victim with your other arm around the victim's waist. If you have another person to help you, he or she can support the victim the same way on the other side.

If you have a second rescuer to help, you can also carry a victim who can't walk. The seat carry provides a secure way for two people to carry a victim. The two rescuers face each other

The clothes drag.

and interlock their arms, each with one arm under the victim's thighs and one arm behind the victim's back. The victim is lifted by the seat formed by the rescuer's arms.

If you are alone and the victim can't walk with assistance, you can drag the victim. Use the victim's clothes (e.g., shirt, coat, or sweater) to drag the victim if you suspect a head or spine injury. Gather the victim's clothes tightly behind the victim's neck. Use the clothes to pull the victim. Support the head with the clothes and your hands.

The walking assist.

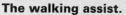

The two-person seat carry.

CALL

While you are checking the victim, use your senses of sight, smell, and hearing. They will help you notice anything abnormal. For example, an unusual smell may be caused by a poison. You may see a bruise or a twisted arm or leg. Listen carefully to what the victim says.

CALL

It is very important that you know your local emergency number. It may be 9-1-1, 0 for operator, a local seven-digit number, or a special response number where you work. Post your emergency number by the phone at home and at work.

Calling for help is often the most important action you can take to help the victim! It will start professional emergency help on its way as fast as possible. Whenever possible, ask a bystander to make the call for you. When possible, tell the caller the victim's condition so that he or she can tell the dispatcher. Tell the caller not to hang up before the dispatcher does. This might cut off some information the

dispatcher needs to have or give. There is no hard, fast rule of when to call your emergency number.

Calling for help is often the most important action you can take to help the victim.

You have to use your own judgment. *In general, the best guideline is: when in doubt . . . call.*

If you are the only person on the scene, shout for help. If the victim is unconscious and no one comes at once to help you, you will need to get professional help fast. Find the nearest telephone as quickly as possible. Make the call and go back to the victim. Recheck the victim and give the necessary care.

If you shout and no one responds while you are giving urgent care, such as controlling severe bleeding, continue for about a minute while you think where to find the nearest telephone. Then get to that telephone as quickly as possible. After making the call, return to the victim.

It is clear that you should call your local emergency number if a victim is unconscious. You should also call if a victim is faint, drowsy, confused, dizzy, or drifts in and out of consciousness.

Call for an ambulance if a victim is having trouble breathing or is breathing in an unnatural way. A victim who is breathing very slowly, heavily, or rapidly, or gasping for breath might not be getting enough air or may stop breathing. A victim who is making rasping, shrill, gurgling, or choking noises may be in similar danger. A victim who has no pulse does not have a beating heart. A victim who is bleeding severely will die after losing a large amount of blood. These are life-threatening conditions requiring the rapid assistance of medical professionals.

Other conditions may be less obvious but no less dangerous. A victim with pain or pressure in the chest or abdomen may well have injuries you can't see—internal injuries—and so may the victim who is vomiting or passing blood.

Seizures, a severe headache, and slurred speech can all be signals of serious injury. The victim may be poisoned, have a head or spinal injury, or have some other dangerous condition, so call. If you suspect the victim has one or more broken bones, call for an ambulance also. If not cared for properly, fractures can cause both immediate and long-term problems.

You also need to call 9-1-1 or your local emergency number for certain situations that must be dealt with only by trained and equipped people. Fire and explosion are situations of this type and so are downed electrical wires and swiftly moving or rapidly rising water. They make a scene unsafe, and you must always stay at a safe distance when any of these conditions are part of an emergency scene.

Poisonous gas can be harder to detect. Sometimes it has no odor or color. You might suspect poisonous gas is present if you see people who are unconscious or behaving strangely for no apparent reason. Call your emergency number. Call also for vehicle collisions and for situations in which victims cannot

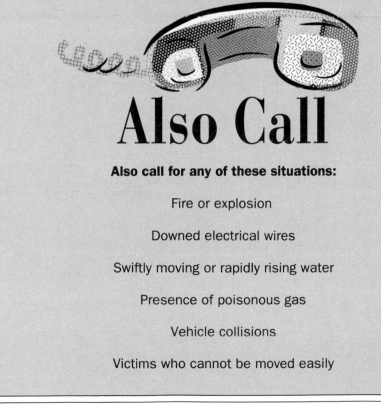

When To Call

EMS

If the victim is unconscious, call 9-1-1 or your local emergency number immediately. Sometimes a conscious victim will tell you not to call an ambulance, and you may not be sure what to do. Call for an ambulance anyway if the victim —

Is or becomes unconscious.

Has trouble breathing or is breathing in a strange way.

Has chest pain or pressure.

Is bleeding severely.

Has pressure or pain in the abdomen that does not go away.

Is vomiting or passing blood.

Has seizures, a severe headache, or slurred speech.

Appears to have been poisoned.

Has injuries to the head, neck, or back.

Has possible broken bones.

Also Call

Also call for any of these situations:

Fire or explosion

Downed electrical wires

Swiftly moving or rapidly rising water

Presence of poisonous gas

Vehicle collisions

Victims who cannot be moved easily

HOW TO

CALL EMS

The most important help that you can provide to a victim who is unconscious or has some other life-threatening emergency is to call professional medical help. Make the call quickly and return to the victim. If possible, send someone else to make the call. Be sure that you or another caller follows these four steps:

1 Call the emergency number. The number is 9-1-1 in many communities. In others, it is a seven-digit number. Dial 0 (the operator) if you do not know the number in the area.

2 Give the dispatcher the necessary information. Answer any questions that he or she might ask. Most dispatchers will ask:

- The exact location or address of the emergency. Include the name of the city or town, nearby intersections, landmarks, the building name, the floor, and the room or apartment number.
- The telephone number from which the call is being made.
- The caller's name.
- What happened — for example, a motor vehicle collision, fire, or fall.
- How many people are involved.
- The condition of the victim(s) — for example, unconsciousness, chest pains, or severe bleeding.
- What help (first aid) is being given.

3 Do not hang up until the dispatcher hangs up. The EMS dispatcher may be able to tell you how to best care for the victim.

4 Return and continue to care for the victim.

With a life-threatening emergency, the survival of a victim often depends on both professional medical help *and* the care you can provide. You will have to use your best judgment, based on knowledge of your surroundings, knowledge gained from this course, and other training you may have received to make the decision to call. Generally, *call FAST!*

WHAT HAPPENS WHEN YOU CALL EMS

When your call is answered, you will be talking to an emergency dispatcher who has had special training in dealing with crises over the phone.

The dispatcher will ask you for your phone number and address and will ask other key questions to determine whether you need police, fire, or medical assistance.

It may seem that the dispatcher asks a lot of questions. The information you give will help the dispatcher to send the type of help you need, based on the severity of the emergency.

Once the ambulance is on the way, the dispatcher may stay on the line and continue to talk with you. Many dispatchers today are also trained to give instructions before EMS arrival, so they can assist you with certain life-saving techniques, such as CPR or rescue breathing, until the ambulance arrives.

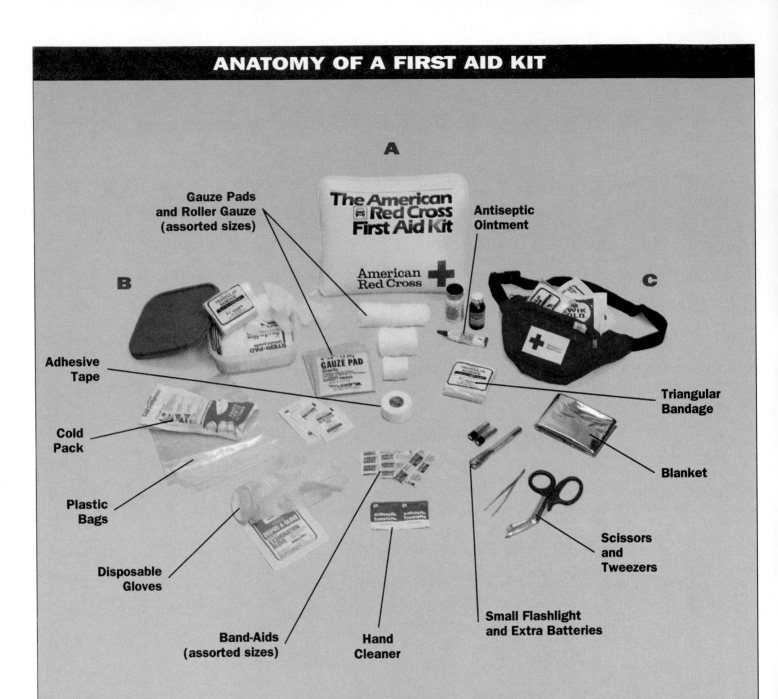

A

**Gauze Pads
and Roller Gauze
(assorted sizes)**

**Antiseptic
Ointment**

B

C

**Adhesive
Tape**

**Triangular
Bandage**

**Cold
Pack**

Blanket

**Plastic
Bags**

**Disposable
Gloves**

**Scissors
and
Tweezers**

**Small Flashlight
and Extra Batteries**

**Band-Aids
(assorted sizes)**

**Hand
Cleaner**

A well-stocked first aid kit is a handy thing to have. To be prepared for emergencies, keep a first aid kit in your home and in your automobile. Carry a first aid kit with you or know where you can find one when you are hiking, biking, camping, or boating. Find out the location of first aid kits where you work.

First aid kits come in many shapes and sizes. **A,** You can buy one from a drug store, or your local Red Cross chapter may sell them. **B,** You can make your own first aid kit. **C,** Some kits are designed for specific activities, such as hiking, camping, or boating. Whether you buy a first aid kit or put one together, make sure it has all the items you may need. Include any personal items, such as medications and emergency phone numbers, or other items your physician may suggest. Check the kit regularly. Make sure the flashlight batteries work. Check expiration dates and replace any used or out-of-date contents.

be reached or moved easily. They may be trapped in cars or in buildings, for example. Call also for emergencies involving more than one victim.

These circumstances aren't a complete list. There are always exceptions. Trust your instincts. If you think there is an emergency, there probably is. If you are confused or unsure about what care to give, call for an ambulance at once. EMS personnel would rather come and find no emergency than arrive at an emergency too late to help.

CARE

Once you have checked the scene and the victim, you may need to provide care. To do this, you can follow some general steps of care. Always care for life-threatening emergencies before those that are not life-threatening. While you are waiting for the ambulance, watch for changes in the victim's breathing and consciousness. Help the victim rest comfortably. Keep him or her from getting chilled or overheated. Reassure the victim.

If the victim is conscious and able to talk, he or she is breathing and has a pulse. Introduce yourself, ask the victim's permission for you to help. Ask what happened and if the victim hurts anywhere. If the victim has pain, ask where the pain is located and what it is like— burning, aching, sharp, stinging. Ask when it started and how bad it

Always care for life-threatening emergencies first!

PROVIDE CARE FOR THE VICTIM

Getting Permission to Give Care

You may want to care for an injured or ill person, but before giving first aid, you must have the victim's permission. To get permission you *must* tell the victim who you are, how much training you have, and how you plan to help. Only then can a conscious victim give you permission to give care.

Do not give care to a conscious victim who refuses it. If the conscious victim is an infant or child, permission to give care should be obtained from a supervising adult when one is available. If the condition is serious, permission is implied if a supervising adult is not present.

Permission is also implied if a victim is unconscious or unable to respond. This means that you can assume that, if the person could respond, he or she would agree to care.

is. Be calm and patient. Speak normally and simply.

After you have finished checking the victim and giving care, you might decide it is OK to take the victim to a hospital or doctor yourself. Be very careful about making this decision. Do not transport a victim with a life-threatening condition or one that could become life-threatening.

A car trip can be painful for the victim. It can also make an injury worse. If you do decide to transport the victim, always have someone else come with you. Watch the victim carefully for any changes in condition. Be sure you know the fastest route. **Do not let the victim drive, either alone or with you.**

When you respond to an emergency, remember the emergency action steps: check, call, and care. They guide your actions in an emergency and ensure your safety and the safety of others. By following these steps, you can give the victim of a serious illness or injury the best chance of survival.

Don't Cry Wolf!

Your local emergency number is for just that—emergencies! It should not be misused. Nonemergency calls account for about 30 to 40 percent of all 9-1-1 calls in many U.S. cities. So please, use good judgment.

DEVELOPING A PLAN OF ACTION

Emergencies can happen quickly. There may be no time to think about what you should do. There may be only enough time to react. You can improve your reaction and change the outcome of the emergency by planning.

Everyone has a plan of action. It may be instinct. It may be as simple as, "I'm scared . . . run!" Running may even work—if you can run fast enough and in the right direction. Most of us do not want to base how well we deal with emergencies on how fast we run. We would rather find a way to improve our chances. We need a well–thought-out plan.

A good plan identifies the emergencies you are most likely to face. The plan also identifies the possible location and the persons involved. All of this information can help you to define the size and scope of a possible emergency. Now, you can begin to decide how you would respond and what other information and training you would need.

The first step in planning is to gather information. Here are some suggestions on where to start.

First, think about your home.
- Type of home (mobile, high rise, duplex, single family, etc.)
- Type of construction (wood, brick, etc.)
- Location of sleeping areas

- Number and location of smoke alarms
- Location of gasoline, solvent, or paint storage
- Number and types of locks on doors
- Location of telephones
- Location of flashlights
- Location of fire extinguisher
- Location of first aid kit

Think about who lives there.
- Number of people living in the home
- Number of people over 65 or under 6 years of age
- Number of people sleeping above or below the ground floor
- Number of people unable to exit without help

Think about the types of emergencies that you may face at home.
- Injuries (like a fall or a cut)
- Illnesses (like a stroke or a heart attack)
- Natural disasters (like a tornado or an earthquake)
- Fire

Now that you have information, you can start to plan.
Get help from the people you live with. Write the list of emergencies and under each emergency, list —
1. The way the emergency would affect your home.
2. The way you would like the people in your home to react.
3. The steps you have taken to prevent or minimize the effect of the emergency.
4. The steps you need to take.

For example, using the information you have, under fire you might list —
1. The fire could burn all or part of our home.
2. If the fire started on the stove while someone was cooking, that person should use a fire extinguisher to put out the fire. If the fire could not be controlled, he or she should call the emergency number, have everyone leave the house, and leave also. Then everyone should meet at the tree in the front yard.
3. Smoke alarms are in the kitchen, the stairwells, and outside the bedrooms. A fire extinguisher is in the kitchen.
4. We should make sure the fire extinguisher is charged and everyone should know how to operate it. We should also make sure everyone knows what to do.

If you need more help, here are other sources of information:
- Insurance companies
- Your city or county Emergency Management office
- Your police department
- Your fire department/rescue squad

Try to imagine as many situations as possible for each emergency. Think about emergencies away from home. Use the same process to decide what to do. When people have questions, others living in the home can help decide what action to take.

When you reach a decision, write it down. You now have a personal plan. Practice it. Keep it current.

FIRST AID CHALLENGE

1.

A 10-year-old child darts onto the road between two parked cars and is struck by an oncoming bicyclist. Both victims are injured on the busy road. What would you do?

2.

You witness your 60-year-old neighbor grasp his chest and suddenly collapse on the ground while doing yard work. He does not appear to be breathing. What would you do?

You have learned the emergency action steps that can be applied in any emergency—check, call, and care. Would you know what to do in an emergency? Test your knowledge of the emergency action steps by deciding what you would do in each of the four situations below. If you are unsure how you should proceed in any of the four situations, review the information in the "Taking Action" article.

3.

Your 50-year-old relative has been complaining of an "unusual tightness" in her chest and nausea for several hours. Suddenly she experiences severe pain in her chest and is now having trouble breathing. What would you do?

4.

A pitcher on a little league baseball team has been struck in the ankle by a line-drive. He falls to the ground in pain and is unable to move his foot. What would you do?

CHECKING

When you reach the victim, check first for life-threatening conditions, such as

unconsciousness. In many emergencies, you will know right away whether the

victim is unconscious. However, in some situations,

you may not be able to tell. If you are not sure

whether a victim is unconscious, tap the victim

on one shoulder.

Always begin by determining if a victim is conscious. To find out if a victim is conscious, tap him or her on one shoulder. Ask the victim if he or she is OK. If you know the person, use his or her name. Speak loudly. If the victim does not respond to you, assume he or she is unconscious. Call for an ambulance at once.

THE VICTIM

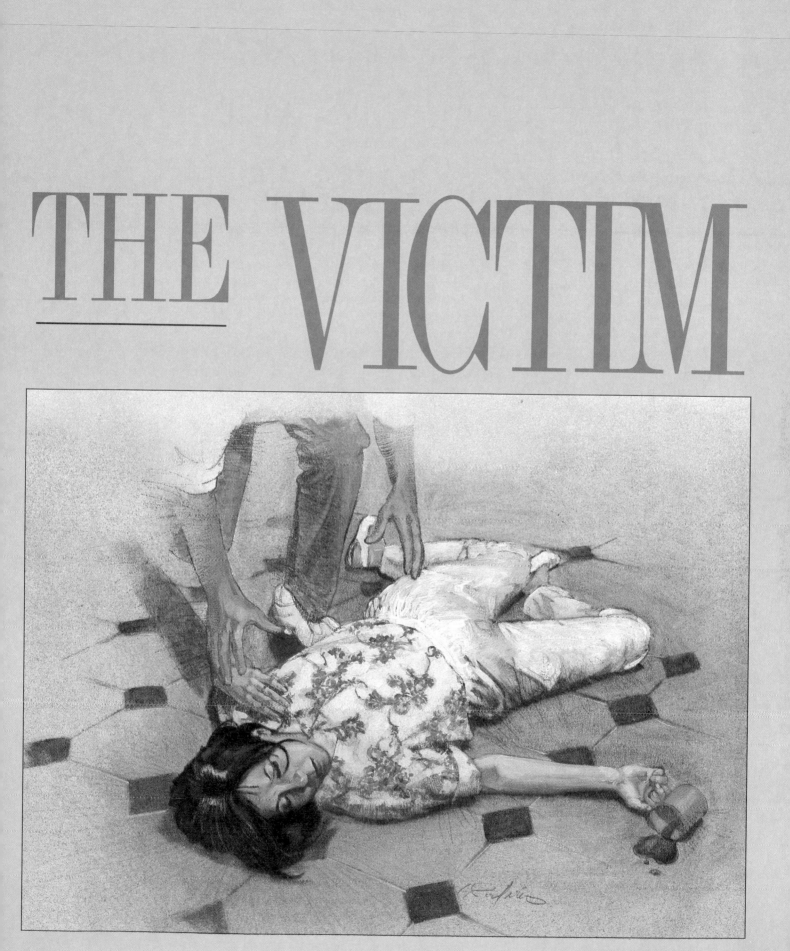

CHECKING AN UNCONSCIOUS VICTIM

After you call for an ambulance, you should return immediately to the victim. If you send another person to call, check the victim while the other person is calling. You must find out if there are other conditions that threaten the victim's life. You should check to see if an unconscious victim—

• Is breathing.
• Has a pulse.
• Is bleeding severely.

If the victim is not breathing, the victim's life is threatened. To check to see if the victim is breathing, put your head near the victim's mouth and nose. Look, listen, and feel for breathing for about 5 seconds. At the same time, watch the chest to see if it rises and falls.

Perhaps the victim isn't in a position where you can do this. For example, the victim may be facedown, and you can't tell whether

If the victim does not respond to you, assume he or she is unconscious. Call for an ambulance at once!

Check to see if an unconscious victim—

■ **Is Breathing.**

■ **Has a Pulse.**

■ **Is Bleeding Severely.**

the victim is breathing. In this case, roll the victim gently onto his or her back. Be sure to keep the head and back in as straight a line as possible while you roll the victim.

Tip the victim's head back and lift the chin, then recheck breathing. If the victim is breathing, the victim's heart is beating and circulating blood. If the victim is not breathing, you must immediately give the victim a couple of breaths. Then find out if the victim's heart is beating by checking the pulse.

To check the pulse in an adult or a child, feel at the front of the neck for the Adam's apple and slide your fingers into the groove next to it in the side of the neck. If the heart is beating, you will feel the

beat of the blood in one of the big blood vessels that run along both sides of the neck. With a baby, feel in the arm midway between the elbow and the shoulder. This beat you feel in the neck or the arm is called the pulse. Take about 5 seconds to feel for the pulse.

If the victim has a pulse but is still not breathing, you will have to do rescue breathing. If the victim does not have a pulse, the heart is not beating properly. You must keep blood circulating in the victim's body until medical help arrives. To do this, you will have to give cardiopulmonary resuscitation, (CPR). Rescue breathing and CPR are discussed in a later article called "When Seconds Count."

To check for breathing, look, listen, and feel for breathing. Watch the chest to see if it rises.

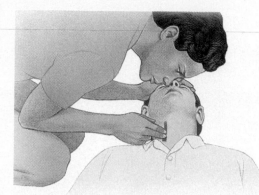

To find out if the heart is beating, check the pulse. Check the pulse of an adult or child at the side of the neck. Check the pulse of an infant at the inside of the arm between the shoulder and the elbow.

Adult

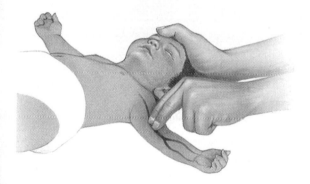

Child

Infant

SKILL SHEET

If the Victim Appears Unconscious...

Check for bleeding by looking over the victim's body from head to toe for signs of bleeding such as blood-soaked clothing. Bleeding is severe, for example, when blood spurts out of a wound. Bleeding usually looks worse than it is. A small amount of blood on a slick surface or mixed with water almost always looks like a great deal of blood. It isn't always easy to recognize severe bleeding. You will have to make a decision based on your best judgment. If you think bleed-ing is severe, call your local emergency number.

CHECKING A CONSCIOUS VICTIM

If the victim is conscious, ask what happened. If the victim is able to speak with you, he or she is breathing and has a pulse. Look for other life-threatening conditions and conditions that need care or might become life-threatening. The victim may be able to tell you what

Check the Victim

STEP 1
Tap and shout to see if the person responds.

If no response ...

STEP 2
Look, listen, and feel for breathing for about 5 seconds.

If the person is not breathing or you can't tell ...

STEP 3
Position victim on back, while supporting head and neck.

STEP 4
Tilt head back and lift chin.

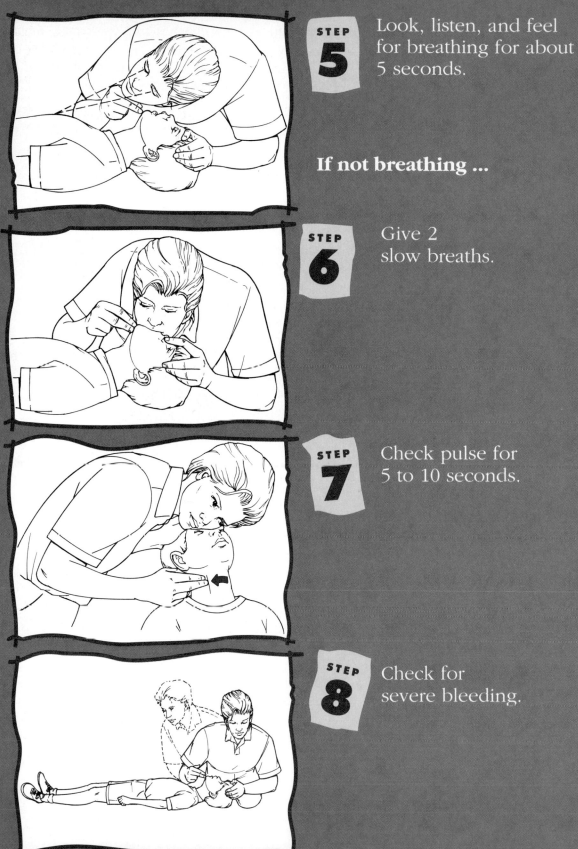

STEP 5 Look, listen, and feel for breathing for about 5 seconds.

If not breathing ...

STEP 6 Give 2 slow breaths.

STEP 7 Check pulse for 5 to 10 seconds.

STEP 8 Check for severe bleeding.

Medical alert tags can provide important medical information about the victim.

happened and how he or she feels. This information helps determine what care may be needed.

This check has two steps:

1. Talk to the victim and to any people standing by who saw the emergency take place.
2. Check the victim from head to toe, so you do not overlook any problems.

Don't ask the victim to move, and do not move the victim yourself. Injured people will find the most comfortable position to be in.

Begin your check at the victim's head, examining the scalp, face, ears, nose, and mouth. Look for cuts, bruises, bumps, or depressions. Watch for changes in consciousness. Notice if the victim is drowsy, not alert, or confused. Look for changes in the victim's breathing. A healthy person breathes regularly, quietly, and easily. Babies and young children normally breathe faster than adults. Breathing that is not normal includes noisy breathing such as gasping for air; making rasping, gurgling, or whistling sounds; breathing unusually fast or slow; and breathing that is painful.

Notice how the skin looks and feels. Note if the skin is reddish, bluish, pale, or gray. Feel with the back of your hand on the forehead to see if the skin feels unusually damp, dry, cool, or hot. The skin can provide clues that the victim is injured or sick.

Look over the body. Ask again about any areas that hurt. Ask the victim to move each part of the body that doesn't hurt. Check the shoulders by asking the victim to shrug them. Check the chest and abdomen by asking the victim to take a deep breath. Ask the victim if he or she can move the fingers,

hands, and arms. Check the hips and legs in the same way. *During a head-to-toe check, don't touch any painful areas; don't ask the victim to move any parts that hurt.* Watch the victim's face for signs of pain and listen for sounds of pain such as gasps, moans, or cries.

Look for odd bumps or depressions. Think of how the body usually looks. If you are not sure if

If a victim is able to talk, you know he or she is breathing and has a pulse.

something is out of shape, check it against the other side of the body.

Look for a medical alert tag on the victim's wrist or neck. A tag will give you medical information about the victim, care to give for that problem, and whom to call for help.

When you have finished checking, if the victim can move his or her body without any pain and there are no other signs of injury, have the victim rest sitting up. When the victim feels ready, help him or her stand up.

As you continue reading, you will learn more about life-threatening emergencies, such as breathing and heart problems.

Changing everyday habits can improve the quality of your life and reduce the possibility of illness and injury. The following list of statements can help you to identify some important steps toward a healthier and safer life. Mark each box next to the statement that represents your actions. Unmarked boxes identify areas that put you at risk.

Stress

- [ ] 1. I plan my days off to allow time for recreation.
- [ ] 2. I get enough sleep.
- [x] 3. I express feelings of anger and worry.
- [ ] 4. I make decisions with little or no worry.
- [ ] 5. I set realistic goals for myself.
- [x] 6. I accept responsibility for my actions.
- [ ] 7. I manage stress so that it does not affect my physical well-being.
- [ ] 8. I discuss problems with friends and relatives.

Physical Health

- [ ] 9. I eat a balanced diet.
- [ ] 10. I have regular medical check-ups.
- [ ] 11. I have regular dental check-ups.
- [ ] 12. I have regular eye examinations.
- [x] 13. I avoid using illegal substances.
- [x] 14. I have fewer than five alcoholic beverages per week.
- [x] 15. I avoid using alcoholic beverages when taking medications.
- [x] 16. When taking medications, I follow the directions on the label.

Personal Safety

- [x] 17. I keep my vehicle in good operating condition.
- [x] 18. I obey traffic laws.
- [x] 19. I wear safety belts whenever I operate my automobile.
- [x] 20. I keep recreational equipment in good working condition.
- [ ] 21. I wear life jackets (personal flotation devices – PFDs) when taking part in water activities, such as boating, fishing, and waterskiing.
- [ ] 22. I swim only when others are present.

Home Safety

- [ ] 23. I post local emergency number(s) near my telephone(s).
- [ ] 24. I have battery-operated smoke detectors where I live.
- [ ] 25. I keep medications safely and securely stored out of the reach of children.
- [ ] 26. I keep cleansers and other poisonous materials safely and securely stored.
- [ ] 27. I turn off the oven and other appliances after use.
- [ ] 28. I keep a working fire extinguisher in my home.
- [ ] 29. I have an emergency plan in the event of injury, sudden illness, or natural disaster.
- [ ] 30. I practice emergency plans with my family or roommates.

WHEN

SECONDS COUNT

In a life-threatening emergency, you must help at once. It may only be a matter of seconds before the person dies. An emergency is life-threatening if the victim is un-conscious, is not breathing, is breath-ing with difficulty, has no pulse, or is bleeding severely.

Fortunately, most of the victims you encounter will be conscious. Very likely, they will be able to in-dicate what is wrong by speaking to you or by gesturing. You will be able to ask them questions. But when a person cannot be aroused, it is difficult to know what is wrong, besides the fact that he or she is unconscious. Unconsciousness is a signal that the victim's life is threatened. You need to have someone call for an ambulance while you continue to check the victim to see if he or she is breathing, has a pulse, or is bleeding severely.

You may have to care for a person who is unconscious but who is breathing normally and has a pulse. For example, a person might have hit his or her head in a fall or just fainted. In such cases, make sure someone has called the local emergency number. There is no need to move the person as long as he or she is breathing adequately. If the person vomits, roll him or her onto one side and clear the mouth and throat. If the person stops breathing, position the person on his or her back and breathe for the person as described later in this article. If you are alone and have to leave the person for any reason, such as to call for help, position the person on the side in case he or she vomits while you are gone.

Most often, unconsciousness is a signal that a victim may have other life-threatening conditions. A person who is unconscious will soon die if breathing stops and if the heart stops. You must discover

0 minutes: Breathing stops. Heart will soon stop beating.

4 - 6 minutes: Brain damage possible.

6 - 10 minutes: Brain damage likely.

Over 10 minutes: Irreversible brain damage certain.

Time is critical in life-threatening emergencies. Unless the brain gets oxygen within minutes of when breathing stops, brain damage or death will occur.

and care for these conditions as quickly as possible.

Breathing Emergencies

The body requires constant oxygen to survive. When you breathe air in through the nose and mouth, it travels down the throat, through the windpipe, and into the lungs. This pathway from the nose and mouth to the lungs is commonly called the airway. Once air reaches the lungs, oxygen in the air is transferred to the blood. The blood transports the oxygen to the brain, and heart, as well as to all other parts of the body.

Certain emergencies are life-threatening because they greatly

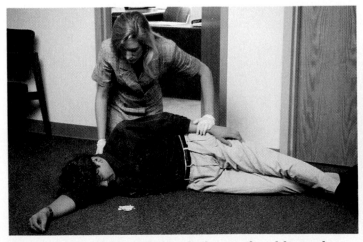

If vomiting occurs, roll the victim on the side, and clear the mouth of any matter.

If you are alone and must leave an unconscious victim, position the person on his or her side in case the person vomits while you are gone.

OXYGEN IS VITAL TO LIFE

The body requires a constant supply of oxygen to survive. When you breathe air in through the nose and mouth, it travels down the throat, through the windpipe, and into the lungs. This path from the nose and mouth to the lungs is called the airway.

When the air you breathe reaches the lungs, oxygen from the air is transferred to the blood and is circulated to all parts of the body through large blood vessels called arteries.

Injuries and illnesses that affect breathing or the action of the heart or cause bleeding can interrupt the supply of oxygen. When enough oxygen does not reach the lungs or does not circulate properly in the body, it is a life-threatening emergency. You must act immediately.

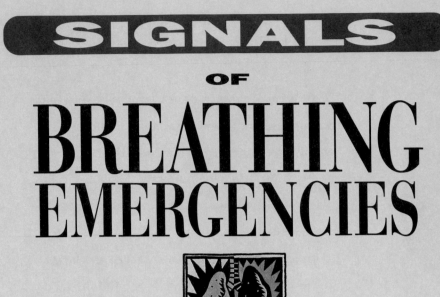

SIGNALS

OF

BREATHING EMERGENCIES

Breathing is unusually slow or rapid.

Breaths are unusually deep or shallow.

Victim is gasping for breath.

Victim is wheezing, gurgling, or making high-pitched noises.

Victim's skin is unusually moist.

Victim's skin has a flushed, pale, or bluish appearance.

Victim feels short of breath.

Victim feels dizzy or light-headed.

Victim feels pain in chest or tingling in hands or feet.

reduce or eliminate the body's supply of oxygen. For instance, when a person has difficulty breathing, that person's body may not get enough oxygen. When breathing stops or when the heart stops, the body gets none. Unless the brain gets oxygen within minutes of when breathing stops, brain damage or death will occur.

A breathing problem so severe that it threatens the victim's life is a breathing emergency. In "Checking the Victim," you learned that you have to check to find out whether an unconscious victim is breathing. You also learned that if the victim is breathing, you must determine if he or she is having difficulty breathing.

Breathing emergencies can be caused by injury or illness. For example, if the heart stops beating, breathing will stop. Choking and injury or disease in areas of the brain that control breathing can disturb or stop breathing. In an unconscious person, a likely reason for breathing to stop is that the tongue falls back in the throat and blocks the airway.

Damage to the muscles or bones of the chest can make breathing painful or difficult. Electric shock and drowning can cause breathing to stop. Severe reactions to certain poisons, drugs, insect stings, and foods can also cause breathing emergencies. Other causes include anxiety, excitement, and conditions such as asthma.

Asthma, for example, is a condition that narrows the air passages. This makes breathing difficult, which is frightening. Asthma may be triggered by a reaction to food, pollen, medications, or insect stings. Emotional distress or physical activity can also bring on an asthma attack. People with asthma can usually control an attack with medication. They may carry this medication with them.

Asthma is more common in children and young adults than in older people. You can often tell when a person is having an asthma attack by the wheezing noises he or she makes when breathing.

Hyperventilation occurs when a person breathes faster than normal. It is often the result of fear or anxiety and is most likely to occur in people who are tense and nervous. However, it can also be caused by head injuries, severe bleeding, or illnesses, such as high fever, heart failure, lung disease, and diabetic emergencies. Asthma and exercise also can trigger hyperventilation.

People who are hyperventilating have rapid, shallow breathing. They feel as if they can't get enough air. Often they are afraid and anxious or seem confused. They may say that they feel dizzy or their fingers and toes feel numb and tingly.

Allergic reactions can also cause breathing problems. At first, the reaction may appear only as a rash and a feeling of tightness in the chest and throat, but this condition can become life-threatening. The victim's face, neck, and tongue may swell, closing the airway.

Severe allergic reactions can be caused by insect stings, certain foods, and medications. People who know they have severe allergic reactions to certain things may have learned to avoid them. They may also carry medication to reverse the reaction. If not cared for at once, severe allergic reaction can become life-threatening.

Even though there are many causes of breathing emergencies, you do not need to know the exact cause of a breathing emergency to care for it. You do need to be able to recognize when a person is having trouble breathing or is not breathing at all.

Sitting can make breathing easier for a person who is having trouble breathing.

If a Person Has Trouble Breathing

Normal breathing is easy and quiet. The person doesn't look as if he or she is working hard or struggling to breathe. The person isn't making noise when breathing. Breaths aren't fast or far apart. Breathing doesn't cause the person pain.

The kind of breathing emergency you are most likely to encounter is a conscious person who is having trouble breathing. You can usually identify a breathing problem by watching and listening to the person's breathing and by asking the person how he or she feels. You should also check the victim's skin appearance.

People with breathing problems may look as if they can't catch

When breathing is too fast, slow, noisy, or painful,

CALL FOR AN AMBULANCE
IMMEDIATELY!

their breath. They may gasp for air. They may appear to breathe faster or slower than normal. Their breaths may be unusually deep or shallow. They may make unusual noises, such as wheezing or gurgling. They may make high-pitched noises in their throats. They may have difficulty talking to you or may not be able to talk at all. Their skin, at first, may be damp and look flushed. Later, it may look pale or bluish because their blood is getting low on oxygen.

People with breathing problems may say they feel dizzy or light-headed. They may feel pain in the chest or tingling in the hands and feet. They may be afraid or anxious.

Recognizing the signals of breathing problems and giving care are often the keys to preventing these problems from becoming more serious emergencies. A breathing problem such as choking can cause the victim to stop breathing entirely. Difficulty breathing can be the first signal of a more serious emergency, such as a heart problem.

If a person is having trouble breathing, help him or her rest in a comfortable position. Usually, sitting is more comfortable than lying down because breathing is easier in that position. If the victim is conscious, check for other conditions. Remember that a person having breathing problems may find it hard to talk. Ask bystanders if they know about the victim's condition. The victim can nod to answer yes-or-no questions. Try to reassure the victim and reduce anxiety. This may make his or her breathing easier.

If the victim is breathing rapidly (hyperventilating) and you are sure it is caused by emotion, such as ex-

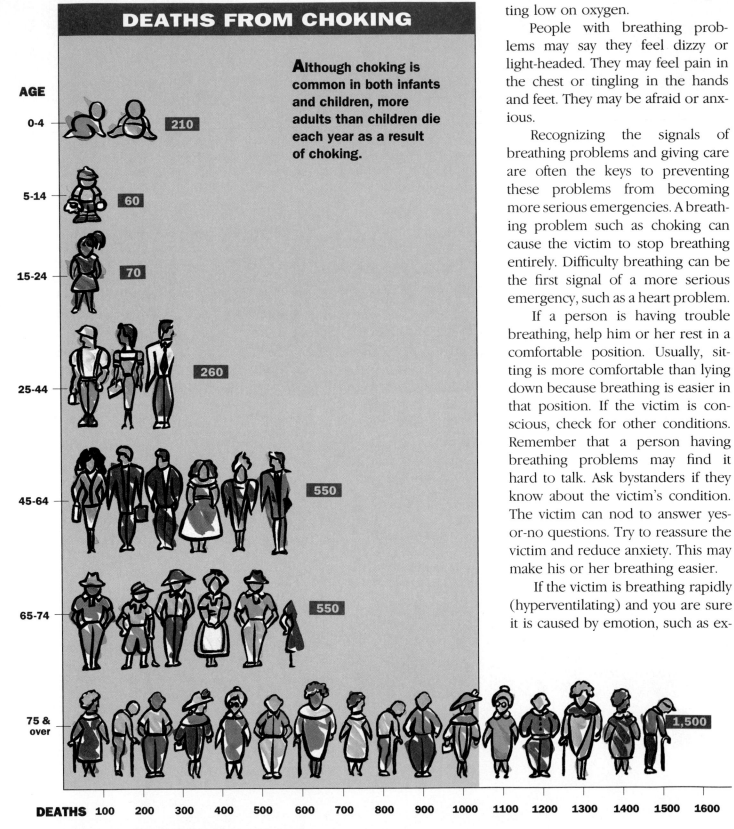

DEATHS FROM CHOKING

Although choking is common in both infants and children, more adults than children die each year as a result of choking.

AGE

0-4 — 210

5-14 — 60

15-24 — 70

25-44 — 260

45-64 — 550

65-74 — 550

75 & over — 1,500

DEATHS   100   200   300   400   500   600   700   800   900   1000   1100   1200   1300   1400   1500   1600

National Safety Council *Accident Facts*, 1991 Edition.

Trying to swallow large pieces of poorly chewed food

Drinking alcohol before or during meals (Alcohol dulls the nerves that aid swallowing.)

Wearing dentures (Dentures make it difficult to sense whether food is fully chewed before it is swallowed.)

Eating while talking excitedly or laughing, or eating too fast

Walking, playing, or running with food or objects in mouth

Common Causes of Choking

citement or fear, tell the victim to relax and breathe slowly. A victim who is hyperventilating from emotion may resume normal breathing if he or she is reassured and calmed down. If the victim's breathing still doesn't slow down, the victim could have a serious problem.

When breathing is too fast, slow, noisy, or painful, call for an ambulance immediately.

If a Person Is Choking

Choking is a common breathing emergency. A conscious person who is choking has the airway blocked by a piece of food or another object. The airway may be partially or completely blocked. A person whose airway is completely blocked can't breathe at all. With a partially blocked airway, the victim is often still able to breathe, although breathing is difficult.

A person with a partially blocked airway can get enough air in and out of the lungs to cough or to make wheezing sounds. The person may also get enough air to speak.

If the choking person is coughing forcefully, let him or her try to cough up the object. A person who

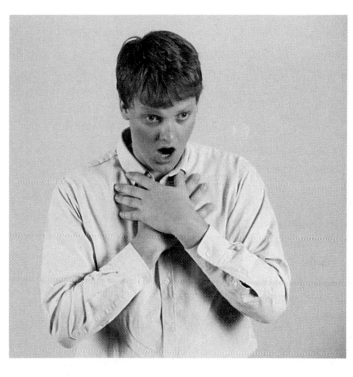

Clutching the throat with one or both hands is universally recognized as a distress signal for choking.

If a choking person is coughing forcefully, encourage him or her to continue coughing.

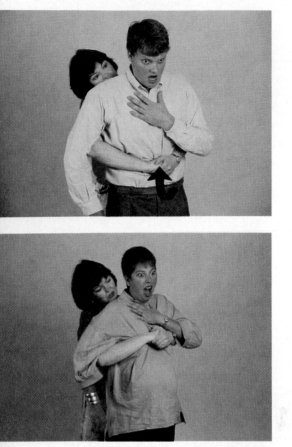

A person who cannot speak, cough forcefully, or breathe is choking. Give quick upward thrusts to the abdomen, just above the navel, until the airway is cleared (*top*). Give chest thrusts when a choking victim is too big for you to reach around or if the victim is noticeably pregnant.

To give yourself abdominal thrusts, press your abdomen onto a firm object, such as the back of a chair.

is getting enough air to cough or speak is getting enough air to breathe. Stay with the person and encourage him or her to continue coughing. However, if the person continues to cough without coughing up the object, call for an ambulance.

A partially blocked airway can very quickly become completely blocked. A person whose airway is completely blocked can't speak, cough forcefully, or breathe. Sometimes the person may cough weakly or make high-pitched noises. This tells you the person isn't getting enough air to stay alive. Act at once! Have a bystander call for an ambulance while you begin to give care.

When someone is choking, you must get the airway open quickly. To do this, give a series of quick, hard thrusts to the victim's abdomen. These abdominal thrusts are also called the Heimlich maneuver. These upward thrusts push the abdomen in, putting pressure on the lungs and airway. This forces the air in the lungs to push the object out of the airway—like the cork from a bottle of champagne.

To give abdominal thrusts, stand behind the victim. Wrap your arms around the victim's waist. Make a fist with one hand and place the thumb side against the middle of the victim's abdomen just above the navel but below the rib cage. Grab your fist with your other hand and give quick, inward and upward thrusts into the abdomen. Repeat these thrusts until the object is forced out or the victim becomes unconscious. If the victim becomes unconscious, follow the procedures for checking an unconscious victim.

If a conscious victim is too big for you to reach around and give effective abdominal thrusts, give chest thrusts. Give chest thrusts to an obviously pregnant victim.

Chest thrusts for a conscious

SKILL SHEET

If Person is Unable to Speak, Cough, or Breathe...

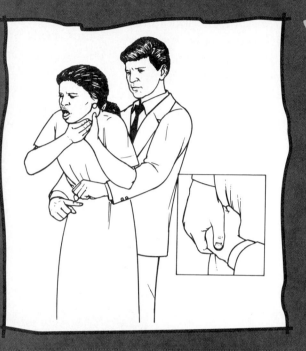

STEP 1

Place thumb side of fist against middle of abdomen just above the navel. Grasp fist with other hand.

STEP 2

Give quick, upward thrusts.

Repeat until object is coughed up or person becomes unconscious.

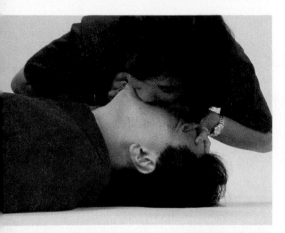

To give rescue breathing, tilt the head back, lift the chin, and pinch the nose shut. Breathe into the victim's mouth.

victim are like abdominal thrusts, except for the placement of your hands. Place your fist against the center of the victim's breastbone. Grab it with your other hand and give quick thrusts into the chest.

If you are alone and choking, you can give yourself abdominal thrusts with your hands. Another option is to lean over and press your abdomen against any firm object such as the back of a chair, a railing, or the kitchen sink. Don't lean over anything with a sharp edge or corner that might hurt you.

If a Person Is Not Breathing

If a person's breathing stops or is restricted long enough, that person will become unconscious, the heart will stop beating, and blood will no longer circulate in the body. Other body systems will quickly fail.

When a person stops breathing, you have to breathe for that person. This is called rescue breathing. It is a way of breathing air into a person that supplies him or her with the oxygen needed to stay alive. Rescue breathing is given to anyone who is unconscious and not breathing but has a pulse.

When a person stops breathing, you have to breathe for that person. This is called

RESCUE BREATHING

A face shield (*top*) or mask (*bottom*), when placed between your mouth and nose and the victim's, can help prevent you from contacting a person's saliva or other body fluids.

WHEN YOU GIVE RESCUE BREATHING,

breathe *slowly* into the victim, only until the chest gently rises.

To give rescue breathing, begin by tilting the head back and lifting the chin to move the tongue away from the back of the throat. This opens the airway, the path that air travels from the nose and mouth to the lungs. Place your ear next to the victim's mouth. Check for breathing by looking at the chest and listening and feeling for breathing for about 5 seconds. If you can't see, hear, or feel any signs of breathing, you must begin to breathe for the victim.

Pinch the victim's nose shut and make a tight seal around the victim's mouth with your mouth. Breathe slowly and gently into the victim until you see the chest rise. Give two breaths, each lasting about 1½ seconds. Pause between breaths to let the air flow out. Watch the victim's chest rise each time you give a breath to make sure your breaths are going in.

Check for a pulse after giving these 2 initial slow breaths. If you feel a pulse but the victim is still not breathing, give one breath about every 5 seconds. You can time the breaths by counting, "one one-thousand, two one-thousand, three one-thousand." Then take a breath on "four one-thousand" and breathe into the victim on "five one-thousand." Counting this way ensures that you give one breath about every 5 seconds. After 10 to 12 breaths, recheck the pulse to make sure the heart is still beating. If the victim has a pulse but is still not breathing, continue rescue breathing. Recheck the pulse about every 10 to 12 breaths. Continue rescue breathing until one of the following happens:

- The victim begins to breathe without your help.
- The victim has no pulse (begin CPR).
- Another trained rescuer takes over for you.
- You are too tired to go on.

You might not feel comfortable with the thought of giving rescue breathing, especially to someone you don't know. Disease transmission is an understandable worry, even though the chances of getting a disease from giving rescue breathing are extremely low. Barriers, such as shields and masks you put between your mouth and nose and the victim's, can help protect you from blood and other body fluids, such as saliva. The devices with one-way valves help protect you from breathing the air the

SKILL SHEET

If Person is Not Breath-ing...

Give Rescue Breathing

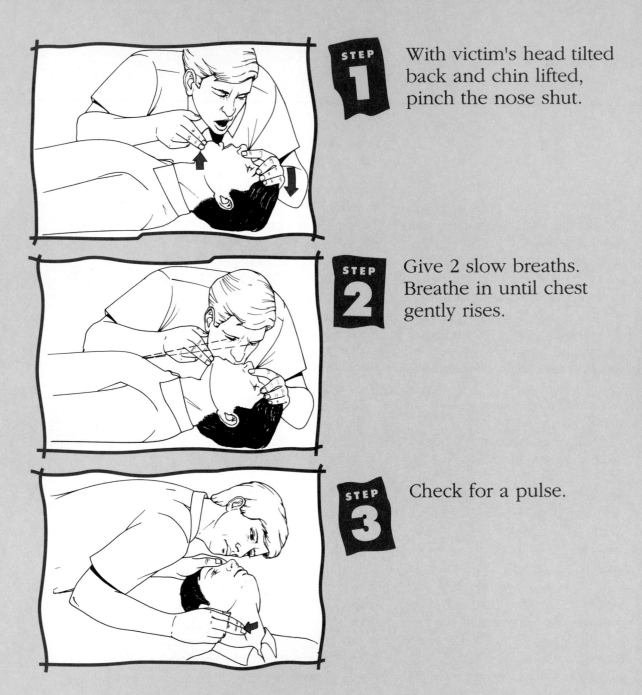

STEP 1
With victim's head tilted back and chin lifted, pinch the nose shut.

STEP 2
Give 2 slow breaths. Breathe in until chest gently rises.

STEP 3
Check for a pulse.

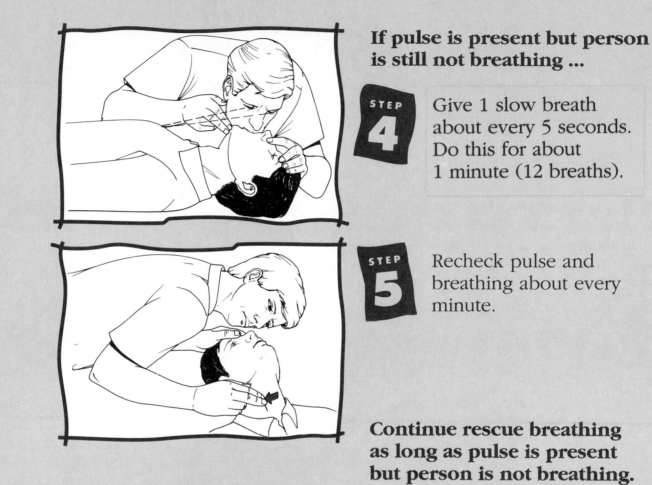

If pulse is present but person is still not breathing ...

STEP 4 Give 1 slow breath about every 5 seconds. Do this for about 1 minute (12 breaths).

STEP 5 Recheck pulse and breathing about every minute.

Continue rescue breathing as long as pulse is present but person is not breathing.

To give mouth-to-nose breathing, keep the head tilted back, close the victim's mouth, and seal your mouth around the victim's nose. Breathe into the nose.

victim exhales. Some devices are small enough to fit in your pocket or in the glove compartment of your car. You can also keep one in your first aid kit.

When you are giving rescue breathing, you want to avoid getting air in the victim's stomach instead of the lungs. This may happen if you breathe too long, breathe too hard, or don't open the airway far enough.

To avoid getting air into the victim's stomach, keep the victim's head tilted back. Breathe *slowly* into the victim, just enough to make the chest rise. Each breath should last about 1½ seconds. Pause between breaths long enough for the air in the victim to come out and for you to take another breath.

Air in the stomach can make the victim vomit. When an unconscious victim vomits, the contents of the stomach can get into the lungs and block breathing. Air in the stomach also makes it harder for the diaphragm, the large muscle that controls breathing, to move. This makes it harder for the lungs to fill with air.

Even when you are giving rescue breathing properly, the victim may vomit. If this happens, turn the victim onto one side and wipe the

mouth clean. If possible, use a protective barrier, such as latex gloves, gauze, or even a handkerchief, when cleaning out the mouth. Then roll the victim on his or her back again and continue with rescue breathing.

Sometimes you may not be able to make a tight enough seal over a victim's mouth. For example, the person's jaw or mouth may be injured or shut too tightly to open or your mouth may be too small to cover the victim's mouth. If you can't make a tight seal, you can breathe into the nose. With the head tilted back, close the mouth by pushing on the chin. Seal your mouth around the victim's nose and breathe into the nose. If possible, open the victim's mouth between breaths to let the air out.

On rare occasions, you may see an opening in a victim's neck as you tilt the head back to check for breathing. This victim may have had an operation to remove part of the windpipe. The victim breathes through this opening, which is called a stoma, instead of through the mouth or nose. This victim will probably also have some medical alert identification, such as a bracelet, identifying this condition. Look, listen, and feel for breathing with

You may need to perform rescue breathing on a victim with a stoma, an opening in the front of the neck *(left)*. To check for breathing, look, listen, and feel for breaths with your ear over the stoma *(middle)*. To give rescue breathing, seal your mouth around the stoma and breathe into the victim *(right)*.

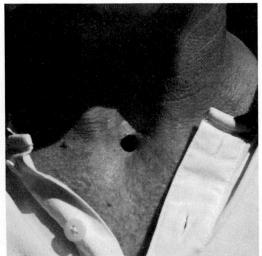

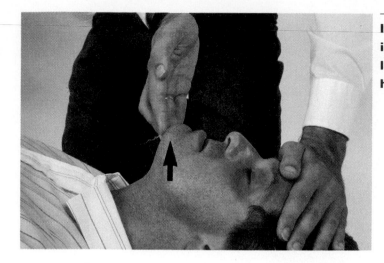

your ear over the stoma. To give rescue breathing to this victim, breathe into the stoma at the same rate as you would breathe into the mouth.

You may have to care for an unconscious person who has nearly drowned. If so, get the person out of the water as quickly as possible. If the victim is not breathing, you will have to breathe for him or her.

Finally, be especially careful when a victim may have a head, neck, or back injury. These can result, for example, from a fall from a height, an automobile collision, or a diving mishap. If you suspect such an injury, try not to move the victim's head and neck. Try to lift the chin without tilting the head when checking breathing and giving rescue breathing. If you are trying to breathe for that person and your breaths don't go in, tilt the head back only slightly. This is all that is usually needed to let air go in. If air still doesn't go in, tilt the head a little more. It is unlikely that tilting the head slightly will further damage the neck. Remember that the nonbreathing victim's greatest need is for air.

If Air Does Not Go In

If you do not see the victim's chest rise and fall as you give

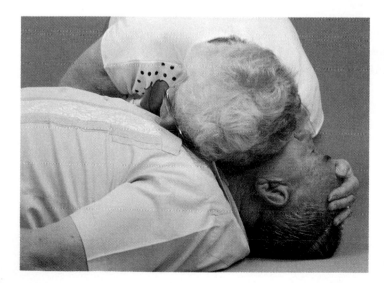 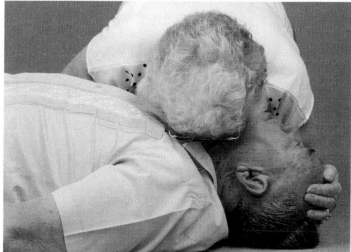

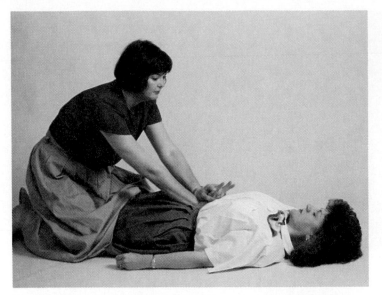

To give abdominal thrusts to an unconscious victim, place the heel of your hands just above the navel with your fingers pointing toward the victim's head and give quick upward thrusts.

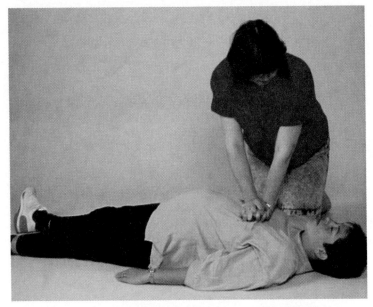

If an unconscious victim is pregnant, give chest thrusts. Kneel to one side of the victim, place the heel of one hand in the center of the breastbone and give quick, downward thrusts.

breaths, you might not have tilted the head far enough back. Retilt the victim's head and repeat the breaths. If your breaths still don't go in, the airway is probably blocked. The airway can become blocked by the tongue falling back in the throat, by food, by an object such as a coin, or by fluids such as blood or saliva.

If you have tried to give 2 slow breaths, retilted the head, and tried again with no success, you must try to clear the airway. This is done by giving up to 5 abdominal thrusts and trying to sweep the object out with your finger.

To give abdominal thrusts to an unconscious victim, straddle one or both of the victim's legs. Place the heel of one hand on the middle of the abdomen just above the navel. Place the other hand on top of the first. Point the fingers of both hands directly toward the victim's head. Give quick thrusts toward the head and into the abdomen.

After giving 5 thrusts, lift the victim's lower jaw and tongue with your fingers and thumb. Slide one finger down the inside of the victim's cheek and try to hook the object out. Be careful not to push it further down. Then reattempt your 2 slow breaths. If you still can't get air into the victim, repeat thrusts, finger sweeps, and breaths. Continue this sequence until the object is removed and you can breathe into the victim.

To give chest thrusts to an unconscious victim whose airway is blocked, kneel to the side of the victim. Place the heel of one hand on the center of the victim's breastbone. Place the other hand on top of it. Give up to 5 quick thrusts. Each thrust should push the chest down about 1½ inches. Then let the chest come up.

Once you are able to get air into the victim, continue to check the victim by feeling for a pulse. If the victim is not breathing, give rescue breathing. If the victim does not have a pulse, give CPR.

Stop giving abdominal or chest thrusts at once if the object comes out or the victim begins to breathe or cough. Make sure the object is out of the airway and watch to see that the person is breathing freely again. Even after the object is coughed up, the person may have breathing problems that you don't notice right away. Also, abdominal thrusts and chest thrusts can cause internal injuries. Therefore, whenever thrusts are used to dislodge an object, the victim should be taken to the nearest hospital emergency department for follow-up care, even if he or she seems to be breathing without difficulty.

SKILL SHEET

If Air Does Not Go In...

IF AN UNCONSCIOUS PERSON IS CHOKING,

it is more important to get air in than to get the object out.

Give Abdominal Thrusts

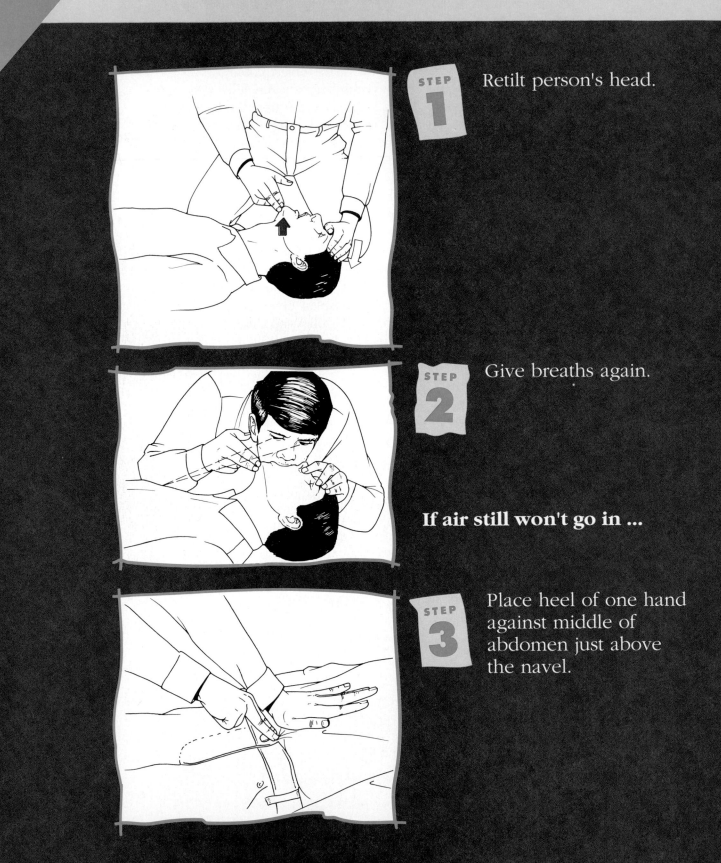

STEP 1
Retilt person's head.

STEP 2
Give breaths again.

If air still won't go in ...

STEP 3
Place heel of one hand against middle of abdomen just above the navel.

STEP 4 Give up to 5 abdominal thrusts.

STEP 5 Lift jaw and tongue and sweep out mouth.

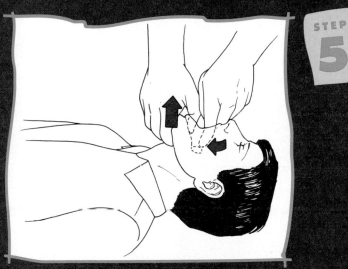

STEP 6 Tilt head back, lift chin, and give breaths again.

Repeat breaths, thrusts, and sweeps until breaths go in.

It is estimated that 66 million Americans suffer some form of cardiovascular disease. Nearly 1 million deaths each year are attributed to cardiovascular disease. Of these, more than half result from heart attacks. The good news is that deaths caused by heart attacks have dropped by over 30 percent and deaths caused by stroke have dropped 50 percent over the past 20 years. An increased awareness of what it means to lead a healthier life has prompted many Americans to make heart-healthy changes in their lives. It is estimated that these changes, including stopping smoking, eating right, and getting regular exercise, have saved as many as 250,000 lives each year.

the HEART of the matter

The heart is a fascinating organ. It beats more than 3 billion times in an average lifetime. The heart is about the size of a fist and lies between the lungs in the middle of the chest. It pumps blood throughout the body. The ribs, breastbone, and the spine protect it from injury. The heart is separated into right and left halves. Blood that contains little or no oxygen enters the right side of the heart and is pumped to the lungs. The blood picks up oxygen in the

lungs when you breathe. The oxygen-rich blood then goes to the left side of the heart and is pumped to all parts of the body.

The heart needs a constant supply of oxygen. Two large blood vessels called arteries supply the heart with oxygen-rich blood. If the heart does not get this blood, it will not work properly. When the heart is behaving normally, it beats evenly and easily, with a steady rhythm. When damage to the heart causes it to stop working effectively, a person experiences a heart attack. A heart attack can cause the heart to beat in an irregular way. This may prevent blood from circulating effectively. When the heart doesn't work properly, normal breathing can be disrupted or stopped. A heart attack can also cause the heart to stop beating entirely. This condition is called cardiac arrest.

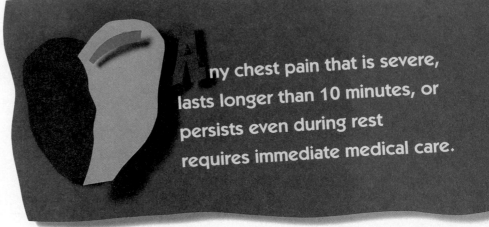

Any chest pain that is severe, lasts longer than 10 minutes, or persists even during rest requires immediate medical care.

Signals of Heart Problems

A heart attack has some common signals. You should be able to recognize these signals so that you can provide proper care.

The major signal is pain or discomfort in the chest that does not go away. Unfortunately, it isn't always easy to tell heart attack pain from the pain of indigestion, muscle spasms, or other conditions. This often causes people to delay obtaining medical care. Brief, stabbing pain or pain that gets worse when you bend or breathe deeply is not usually caused by a heart problem.

The pain associated with a heart attack can range from discomfort to an unbearable crushing sensation in the chest. The victim may describe it as pressure, squeezing, tightness, aching, or heaviness in the chest. Often the victim feels pain in the center of the chest. It may spread to the shoulder, arm, neck, jaw, or back. The pain is constant. It is usually not relieved by resting, changing position, or taking medicine. Any chest pain that is severe, lasts longer than 10 minutes, or persists even during rest requires medical care at once.

Another signal of a heart attack is difficulty breathing. The victim may be breathing faster than normal because the body tries to get much-needed oxygen to the heart. The victim's skin may be pale or bluish, especially around the face. The face may also be damp with sweat. Some heart attack victims

The right side receives oxygen-poor blood (blue) from the body and sends it to the lungs where it picks up oxygen. The left side receives oxygen-rich blood (red) from the lungs and pumps it out through the body. One-way valves direct the flow of blood through the heart.

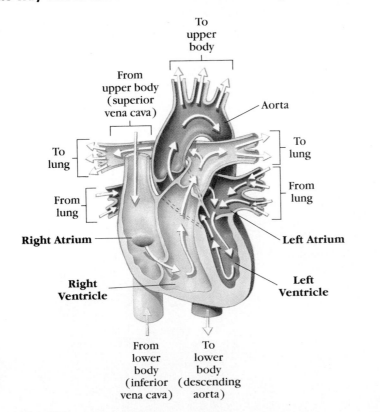

To upper body

From upper body (superior vena cava)

Aorta

To lung

To lung

From lung

From lung

Right Atrium

Left Atrium

Right Ventricle

Left Ventricle

From lower body (inferior vena cava)

To lower body (descending aorta)

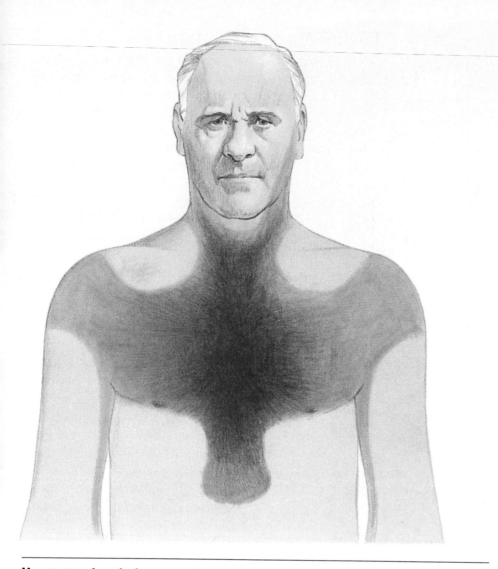

Heart attack pain is most often felt in the center of the chest, behind the breastbone. It may spread to the shoulder, arm, or jaw.

Persistent chest pain or discomfort

Victim has persistent pain or pressure in the chest that is not relieved by resting, changing position, or oral medication. Pain may range from discomfort to an unbearable crushing sensation.

Breathing difficulty

Victim's breathing is noisy. Victim feels short of breath. Victim breathes faster than normal.

Changes in pulse rate

Pulse may be faster or slower than normal or may be irregular.

Skin appearance

Victim's skin may be pale or bluish in color. Victim's face may be moist, or victim may sweat profusely.

sweat heavily. These signals are caused by the stress put on the body when the heart does not work as it should.

Some people with heart disease may have chest pain or pressure that comes and goes. This type of pain is called angina pectoris, a medical term for pain in the chest. It develops when the heart needs more oxygen than it gets because the arteries leading to the heart are too narrow. When a person with angina is exercising, excited, or emotionally upset, the heart might not get enough oxygen. This lack of oxygen can cause chest pain.

Unlike the pain of a heart attack, the pain associated with angina rarely lasts more than 10 minutes. A person who knows he or she has angina may tell you so. Individuals with angina usually have medicine to take to stop the pain. Stopping physical activity or easing the distress and taking the medicine usually stops the pain of angina.

It is important to recognize the signals of a heart attack and act on them. Any heart attack may lead to cardiac arrest! Prompt action may prevent it. A heart attack victim whose heart is still beating has a far

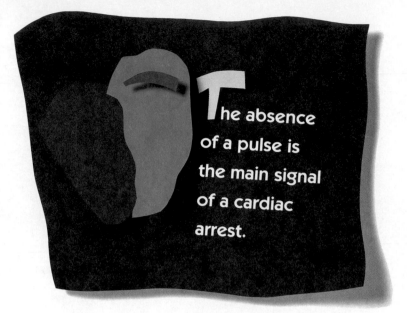

The absence of a pulse is the main signal of a cardiac arrest.

better chance of living than one whose heart has stopped. Most people who die of heart attack die within 2 hours after the first signals appear. Many could have been saved if people on the scene or the victim had been aware of the signals and acted promptly. Early treatment with certain medications, for example, can help minimize damage to the heart after a heart attack.

Many heart attack victims delay getting care. Nearly half of them wait for 2 hours or more before going to the hospital. Often they do not realize they are having a heart attack. They may say the signals are just muscle soreness or indigestion.

Remember, the key signal of a heart attack is chest pain that does not go away. If the pain is severe or does not go away in 10 minutes, call for an ambulance at once. A heart attack victim will probably deny that any signal is serious. Do not let this influence you. If you think the victim might be having a heart attack, you must act quickly. Call your emergency number!

Care for a Heart Attack

Recognize the signals of a heart attack.

Convince the victim to stop activity and rest.

Help the victim to rest comfortably.

Try to obtain information about the victim's condition.

Comfort the victim.

Call the local emergency number for help.

Assist with medication, if prescribed.

Monitor vital signs.

Be prepared to give CPR if the victim's heart stops beating.

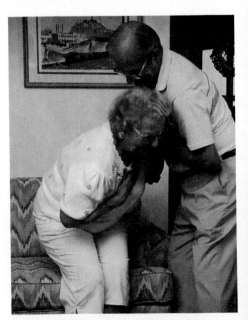

Have a victim with severe chest pain stop and rest. Many victims find it easier to breathe while sitting.

In Case of a Heart Attack

Whenever you suspect that a person is having a heart attack, have the victim stop whatever he or she is doing and rest. Many heart attack victims find it easier to breathe while sitting. Talk to bystanders and the victim, if possible, to learn more. If the victim is having persistent chest pain, ask the victim when the pain started. Ask what brought the pain on, if anything lessens it, what it feels like, and where it hurts.

Ask the victim if he or she has a history of heart disease. Some people with heart disease have medicine to take for it. You can help by getting the medicine for the victim. If you still think the victim may be having a heart attack or if you aren't sure, call for an ambulance. Have a bystander call, or make the call yourself if you're alone. To survive a heart attack, a person needs advanced medical care just as soon as possible! Call your local emergency number before the victim gets worse and the heart stops.

Be calm and reassuring when caring for a heart attack victim. When you comfort the victim, it helps make him or her less anxious and more comfortable. Watch carefully for any changes in the way the victim looks and behaves. Since the victim may go into cardiac arrest, be prepared to give cardiopulmonary resuscitation (CPR).

When the Heart Stops Beating

When the heart stops beating or beats too poorly to circulate blood properly, it is called cardiac arrest. When cardiac arrest happens, breathing soon stops. Cardiac arrest is life-threatening. Every year, more than 300,000 victims die of cardiac arrest before they reach a hospital.

Heart disease is the most common cause of cardiac arrest. Other causes include drowning, choking, and certain drugs. These causes, as well as severe injury brain damage, and severe electric shock, can cause the heart to stop. Cardiac arrest can happen suddenly, without the signals usually seen in a heart attack.

A person in cardiac arrest is unconscious, is not breathing, and has no pulse. The absence of a pulse is the main signal of cardiac arrest. No matter how hard you try, you won't be able to find a pulse. No pulse means no blood is going to the brain. Since blood carries oxygen, no oxygen is going to the brain and the brain will die.

Even though a victim is not breathing and has no pulse, the cells of the brain and of other important organs continue to live for a short time—until the oxygen in the blood is used up. Such a victim needs CPR at once. CPR is a combination of chest compressions and

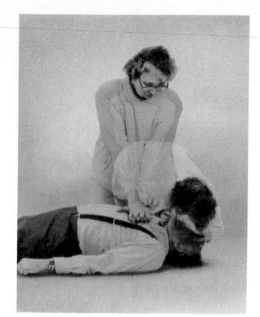

If a victim is not breathing and has no pulse, he or she needs CPR. CPR is a combination of chest compressions and rescue breathing.

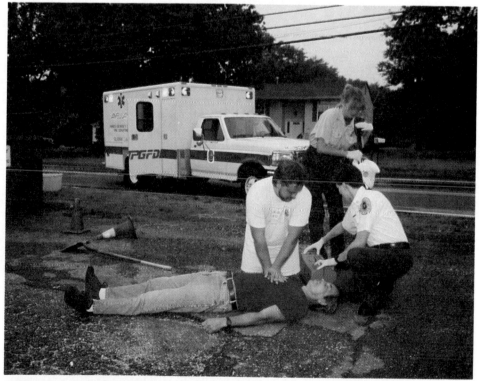

CPR alone is not enough to help someone survive cardiac arrest. Advanced medical care is needed as soon as possible.

rescue breathing. As you read earlier, rescue breathing supplies oxygen. The presence of a pulse means that the heart is circulating this oxygen to the body through the blood. When the heart isn't beating, chest compressions are needed to circulate the oxygen. Given together, rescue breathing and chest compressions take over for the heart and lungs. CPR increases a cardiac arrest victim's chances of survival by keeping the brain supplied with oxygen until the victim can get medical care. Without CPR, the brain begins to die in as little as 4 minutes.

However, CPR provides only about one third the normal blood flow to the brain. CPR alone is not enough to help someone survive cardiac arrest. Advanced medical care is needed as soon as possible. This is why it is so important to call for an ambulance immediately! Trained emergency personnel can provide special care for cardiac arrest. They can use a device called a defibrillator, which sends an electric shock through the chest. The shock enables the heart to begin beating properly again. They can also give medication.

A Matter of Choice

Your 75-year-old grandfather is living with your family. He has a terminal illness and is frequently in the hospital. He has no hope of regaining his health.

One afternoon, you go to his room to give him lunch. As you start to talk to him, you realize he has stopped breathing. You check for a pulse. He has none. You are suddenly faced with the fact that your grandfather is no longer alive . . . he's dead. You ask yourself . . . What do I do?

No one can tell you what to do. No one can advise you. No one can predict the outcome. The decision to try to help your grandfather by giving CPR is a personal one that you must make.

Your mind tells you to give CPR, yet your heart tells you not to. Various questions race through your mind. Can I face the fact I am losing someone I love? Shouldn't I always try to give CPR? What would his life be like after resuscitation? What would grandfather want?

It is important to realize that it is OK to withhold CPR when a terminally ill person is dying. Nature takes its course, and, in some cases, people feel they have lived full lives and are prepared for death. Talking to your grandfather about preferences *before* a crisis occurs can help you with such decisions.

How would this situation have changed if your family and grandfather had planned for this possibility? For instance, what would have happened if your grandfather had given instructions in advance?

Instructions that describe a person's wishes about medical treatment are called advance directives. These instructions are used when the person can no longer make his or her own health-care decisions. If your grandfather is able to make decisions, advance directives do not interfere with his right to do so.

As provided by the federal Patient Self-Determination Act, adults who are admitted to a hospital or a health-care facility or who receive assistance from certain organizations that receive funds from Medicare and

A person in cardiac arrest needs defibrillation as soon as possible. A person has the best chance of surviving cardiac arrest if a bystander gives CPR at once and EMS personnel follow up rapidly with defibrillation.

It is very important to start CPR promptly and continue it until EMS personnel arrive. Any delay in calling for an ambulance and starting CPR makes it less likely the victim will survive. Remember, you are the first link in the victim's chain of survival.

No one is exactly sure how chest compressions work. It is generally thought that chest compressions create pressure in the chest that causes blood to circulate through the body. For compressions to be most effective, the vic-

Medicaid have the right to make fundamental choices about their own care. They must be told about their right to make decisions about the level of life support that would be provided in an emergency situation. They would be offered the opportunity to make these choices at the time of admission.

Verbal conversations with relatives, friends, or physicians, while the patient is still capable of making decisions, are the most common form of advance directives. However, because conversations may not be recalled accurately, the courts consider written directives more trustworthy.

Two examples of written advance directives are living wills and durable powers of attorney for health care. The types of health-care decisions covered by these documents vary depending on where you live. Talking with a legal professional can help determine which advance directive options are available in your state and what they do and do not cover.

If your grandfather had established a living will, directions for health care would be in place before he became unable to communicate his wishes. The instructions that can be included in this document vary from state to state. A living will generally allows a person to refuse only medical care that "merely prolongs the process of dying," such as with a terminal illness.

If your grandfather had established a durable power of attorney for health care, the document would authorize someone to make medical decisions for him in any situation in which he could no longer make them for himself. This authorized person is called a *health care surrogate* or *proxy*. This surrogate, with the information given by the patient's physician, may consent to or refuse medical treatment on the patient's behalf. In this case, he or she would support the needs and wishes that affect the health-care decisions and the advance directives of your grandfather.

A doctor could formalize your grandfather's preferences by writing "Do Not Resuscitate" (DNR) orders in your grandfather's medical records. Such orders would state that if your grandfather's heartbeat or breathing stops, he should not be resuscitated. The choice in deciding on DNR orders may be covered in a living will or in the durable power of attorney for health care.

Appointing someone to act as a health care surrogate along with writing down your instructions is the best way to formalize your wishes about medical care.

Some of these documents can be obtained through a personal physician, attorney, or various state and health-care organizations. A lawyer is not always needed to execute advance directives. However, if you have any questions concerning advance directives, it is wise to obtain legal advice.

Copies of advance directives should be provided to all personal physicians, family members, and the person chosen as the health care surrogate. Tell them what documents have been prepared and where the original and other copies are located. Discuss the docu-

ment with all parties so they understand the intent of all requests. Keep these documents updated.

Keep in mind that advance directives are not limited to elderly people or people with terminal illnesses. Advance directives should be considered by anyone who has decided the care he or she would like to have provided. An unexpected illness or injury could create a need for decisions at any time.

Knowing about living wills, durable powers of attorneys for health care, and DNR orders can help you prepare for difficult decisions. If you are interested in learning more about your rights and the options available to you in your state, contact a legal professional.

REFERENCES
1. Hospital Shared Services of Colorado, Stockard Inventory Program. *Your Right to Make Health Care Decisions*. Denver, Colorado, 1991.
2. Title 42 United States Code, Section 1395 cc (a)(1)(Q)(A) Patient Self-Determination Act.

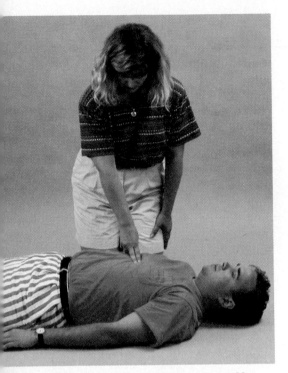

To give CPR, position yourself so that you can give rescue breaths and chest compressions without having to move.

tim should be lying flat, on his or her back, and on a level surface. If a person is in bed, move the person to the floor. CPR doesn't work as well if the victim is sitting up or is on a soft surface like a mattress.

After determining that a victim does not have a pulse, begin chest compressions and rescue breathing. To give chest compressions, kneel beside the victim. Place yourself midway between the head and the chest in order to move easily from giving compressions to giving breaths. Lean over the chest and position your hands. The correct hand and body position lets you give the most effective compressions without tiring you too quickly.

To find the correct hand position, find the notch at the lower end of the victim's breastbone where the ribs meet the breastbone. Place the heel of one hand above this notch. Place your other hand directly on top of it. Try to keep your fingers off the chest by

When to stop CPR

If another trained person takes over CPR for you.

If EMS personnel arrive and take over care of the victim.

If you are exhausted and unable to continue.

If the scene becomes unsafe.

The Shock of Your Life

Every year, 300,000 to 400,000 Americans collapse in their homes, in workplaces, or on the streets as a result of cardiac arrest. Ninety-five percent do not survive, but a simple, new, computerized device offers an increased chance for survival.

In two thirds of all cardiac arrests the heartbeat flutters wildly before it stops. The electric signals that tell the heart muscle to beat stops making sense. The heart is unable to send enough blood through the body. This condition is called ventricular fibrillation and can only be corrected by an electric shock.

Devices that could shock the heart into pumping effectively began to appear in 1966. These devices, called defibrillators, allowed medical personnel, away from the hospital, to monitor the heart's electrical activity. A doctor attached electrodes to the victim's chest to determine the heart's rhythm. If necessary, medical personnel delivered an electric shock to the heart to try to restore the heart's proper rhythm. In addition to doctors, paramedics eventually began to evaluate rhythms and deliver shocks at the emergency scene. Because of the expense and the lack of trained personnel across the United States, victims were not always able to get the lifesaving help that they needed.

Today a new, easy-to-use Automatic External Defibrillator (AED) allows emergency personnel and even citizen responders to provide the lifesaving shocks. The new defibrillators use a computer chip, rather than a medical professional, to analyze the heart's rhythm and deliver a shock if necessary. Typically, the user places two electrodes on the victim's chest. First the user presses the "Analyze" button, then, if the machine prompts the user, he or she presses the "Shock" button. The machine does the rest.

Many first responders, like fire fighters and police officers, are trained to use AEDs. They can reduce the amount of time it takes to give a shock in a cardiac emergency because they are often the first people on the scene. By training the first responders, communities increase the number of emergency personnel trained to use AEDs. In Eugene and Springfield, Oregon, authorities placed AEDs on every fire truck and trained all fire fighters to use them. The survival rates for cardiac arrest in these communities increased by 18 percent in the first year.

More than half of the states recognize defibrillator training for emergency medical technicians (EMTs). Authorities are also placing AEDs in areas where large groups of people gather, such as convention centers, stadiums, large businesses, and industrial complexes. Some experts hope that eventually AEDS will be as commonplace as fire alarms.

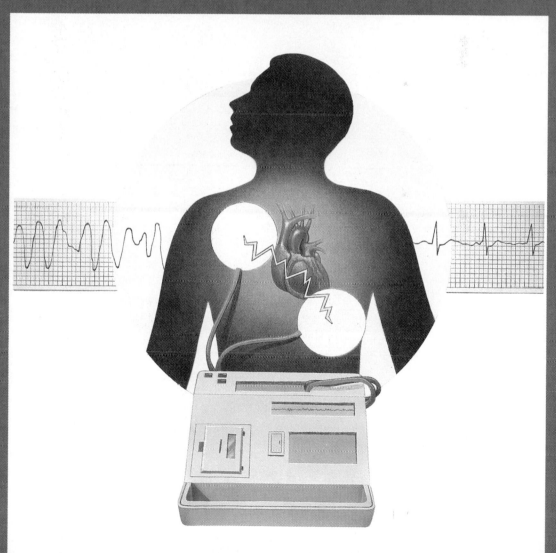

To find hand position, find the notch where the lower ribs meet the breastbone *(top)*. Place the heel of your hand on the breastbone, next to your index finger *(middle)*. Place your other hand on top of the first. Use the heel of your bottom hand to apply pressure on the breastbone *(bottom)*.

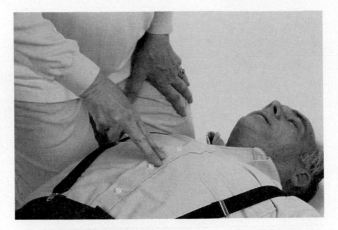

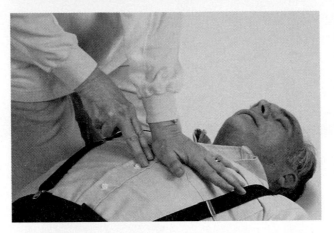

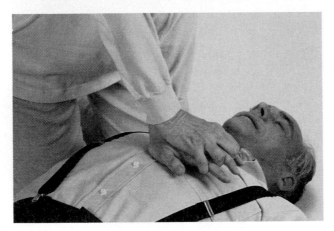

twining them together or sticking them out. If you have arthritis or a similar condition in your hands or wrists, you can give compressions while grasping the wrist of the hand positioned on the chest with your other hand.

Compress the chest by pressing down. Then release. You give chest compressions straight down in a smooth, even rhythm. Keep your shoulders directly over your hands and your elbows locked. Locking your elbows keeps your arms straight and prevents you from tiring quickly.

When you press down, the weight of your upper body creates the force you need to compress the chest. Push with the weight of your upper body, not with your arm muscles. Push straight down; don't rock. Each compression should push the chest down about 2 inches. After each compression, release the pressure on the chest without letting your hands lose contact with the chest. Allow the chest to return to its normal position before you give the next compression.

Keep a steady down-and-up rhythm and don't pause between compressions. Spend half the time going down and half coming up. If your hands slip, find the correct position again. Try not to move them off the chest or change their position.

As you do compressions, count "one and two and three and four and five and six and. . ." You should do 15 compressions in about 10 seconds. That's a little more than one compression per second.

Give 15 compressions, then retilt the head, lift the chin, and give 2 slow breaths. This cycle of 15 compressions and 2 breaths takes about 15 seconds.

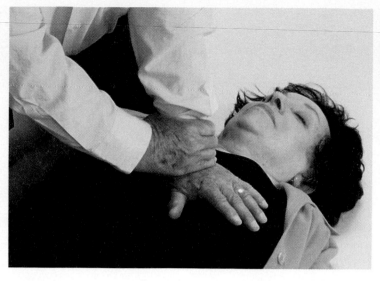

Grasping the wrist of the hand positioned on the chest is an alternate hand position for giving chest compressions.

Do four continuous cycles of CPR, which should take about 1 minute. Check the pulse at the end of the fourth cycle. If there is still no pulse, continue CPR. Check the pulse again every few minutes. If you find a pulse, check the victim's breathing. Give rescue breathing if necessary. If the victim is breathing, keep the head tilted back and check breathing and pulse until an ambulance arrives.

If another person at the scene says he or she knows how to do CPR, one of you should call for an ambulance while the other gives CPR. Then one of you can take over when the other one gets tired. To do this, the first rescuer stops at the end of a cycle of 15 compressions

If Person is Not Breath-ing and Has No Pulse...

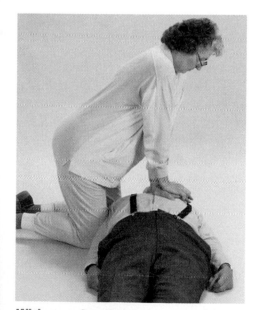

With your hands in place, position yourself so that your shoulders are directly over your hands and your elbows are locked. Press the chest down and then release it, keeping a smooth, even rhythm.

Give CPR

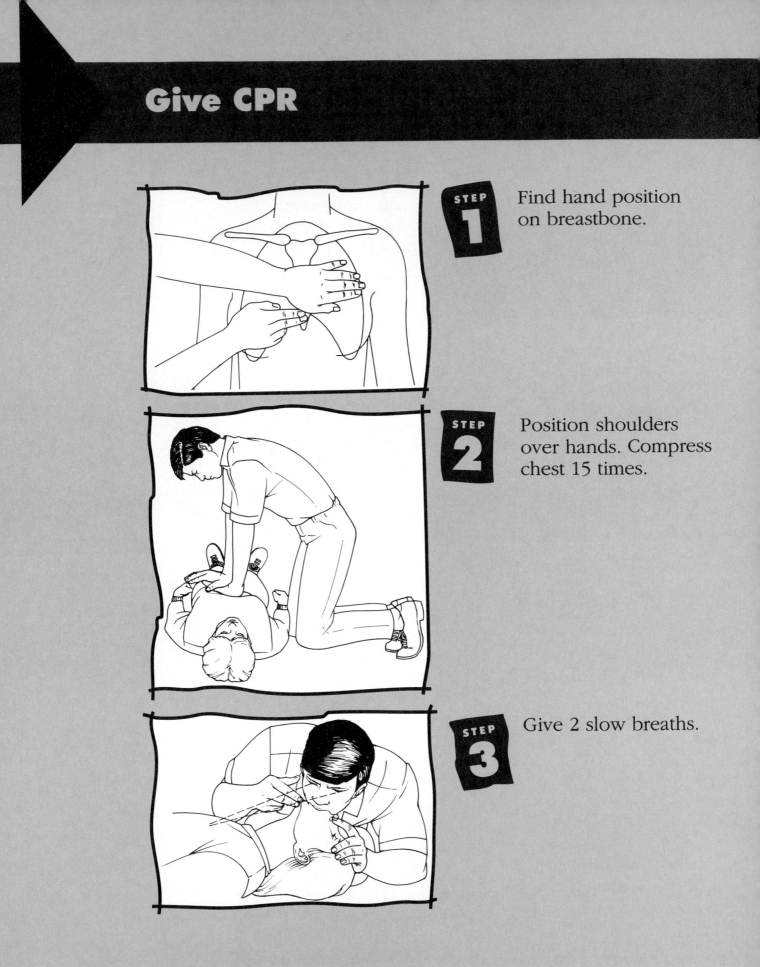

STEP 1 Find hand position on breastbone.

STEP 2 Position shoulders over hands. Compress chest 15 times.

STEP 3 Give 2 slow breaths.

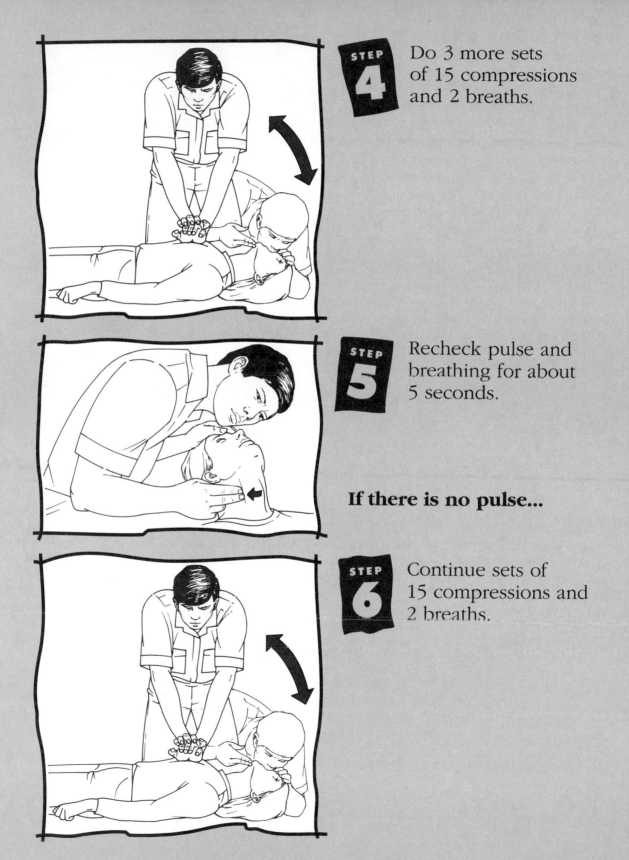

STEP 4 Do 3 more sets of 15 compressions and 2 breaths.

STEP 5 Recheck pulse and breathing for about 5 seconds.

If there is no pulse...

STEP 6 Continue sets of 15 compressions and 2 breaths.

The Brain Speaks

ALL SYSTEMS GO!

Our brains speak to our bodies through a complex system of nerves, cells, and chemicals. In a healthy, well-functioning body this communication process allows us to swim, enjoy music, or tell a joke. However, when the brain does not get enough oxygen to its cells, some may die and cause brain damage, paralysis, or even death.

A disruption of blood flow to a part of the brain that is serious enough to damage brain tissue is called a stroke or a cerebrovascular accident (CVA). In the United States, about 150,000 people die each year because of strokes. Most are over the age of 65.

Stroke is usually caused by a blood clot that forms or lodges in the arteries that supply blood to the brain. Another common cause is bleeding from a damaged artery in the brain. A head injury, high blood pressure, a weak area in an artery wall, or fat deposits lining an artery may cause stroke. A tumor or swelling from a head injury may compress an artery and cause a stroke.

A transient ischemic attack (TIA) is sometimes called a "mini-stroke." Like a stroke, a TIA is caused by reduced blood flow to part of the brain. Unlike a stroke, the signals of a TIA disappear shortly, but the person is not out of danger. Someone who has a TIA has nearly 10 times greater chance of having a stroke in the future. Since you cannot tell a stroke from a TIA, you should call for an ambulance for any stroke-like signals.

If you suspect that someone has had a stroke or a TIA, call for an ambulance immediately. If there is fluid or vomit in the victim's mouth, position him or her on one side to allow any fluids to drain out of the mouth. You may have to remove some of the material from the mouth.

If the person is conscious, offer comfort and reassurance. Often he or she does not understand what has happened. Have the person rest in a comfortable position. Do not give the person anything to eat or drink. If the victim is drooling or having trouble swallowing, place him or her on one side to help drain any fluid from the mouth.

Ten years ago, a stroke almost always caused permanent brain damage. Today, new drugs and medical procedures can limit or, in some cases, reduce the damage caused by stroke. Therefore the sooner you call for an ambulance, the better the victim's chances are for a good recovery.

Preventing Stroke

Risk factors for stroke and TIA are similar to those for heart disease. Some risk factors are beyond your control, such as age, gender, or family history of stroke, TIA, diabetes, or heart disease.

You can control other risk factors. Most important, if you have high blood pressure, talk with your doctor about ways to keep it down. High blood pressure increases your risk of stroke about seven times. High blood pressure puts pressure on arteries and makes them more likely to burst. Even mild high blood pressure can increase your risk of stroke.

Cigarette smoking is another major risk factor for stroke. It increases blood pressure and makes blood more likely to clot. If you don't smoke, don't start. If you do, get help to stop.

A diet high in saturated fats and cholesterol increases your chance of stroke by increasing the possibility of fatty materials building up on the walls of your blood vessels. Eat these foods in moderation.

Regular exercise reduces your chances of stroke by increasing blood circulation, which develops more channels for blood flow. These additional channels provide alternate routes for blood if the primary channels become blocked.

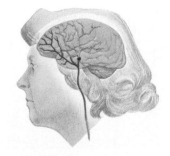
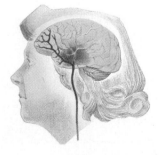

REFERENCES
National Safety Council. *Accident Facts.* Chicago, IL, 1991.

and 2 breaths. The second rescuer checks for breathing and pulse. If there is still no pulse, the second rescuer continues CPR.

Preventing Heart Disease

Recognizing a heart attack and getting the necessary care at once may prevent a victim from going into cardiac arrest. However, preventing a heart attack in the first place is even more effective. There is no substitute for prevention. Heart attacks are usually the result of disease of the heart and blood vessels. Heart disease is the leading cause of death for adults in the United States. It accounts for nearly 1 million deaths each year.

Heart disease develops slowly. Deposits of cholesterol, a fatty substance made by the body and present in certain foods, build up on the inner walls of the arteries. The arteries gradually narrow. As the arteries that carry blood to the heart get narrower, less oxygen-rich blood flows to the heart. This reduced oxygen supply to the heart can eventually cause a heart attack. When arteries in the brain narrow, a stroke can result.

Although a heart attack may seem to strike suddenly, many people live lives that are gradually putting their hearts in danger from heart disease. Because heart disease develops slowly, victims may not be aware of it for many years. Fortunately, it is possible to slow the progress of heart disease by making life-style changes.

Behavior that can harm the heart and blood vessels may begin in early childhood. We may develop a taste for "junk food," which is high in cholesterol but has little

Arteries of the heart

The arteries of the heart supply the heart muscle with blood. A buildup of materials on the inner walls of these arteries reduces the flow of oxygen-rich blood to the heart muscle, causing part of the heart to die. This is called a heart attack.

Unblocked

Partially blocked

Completely blocked

real food value. Heart disease can begin in the teens if those are the years when people begin to smoke. Smoking contributes to heart disease and to other diseases.

Many things increase a person's chances of developing heart disease. These are called risk factors. Some of them you can't change. For instance, men have a higher risk of heart disease than women. A history of heart disease in your family also increases your risk.

Many risk factors can be controlled, however. Smoking, eating a lot of fats, having high blood pressure, being overweight, and taking too little exercise all put you at greater risk of heart disease. When you combine one risk factor, like smoking, with others, such as high blood pressure and not enough exercise, your risk of heart attack or stroke is much greater.

People are becoming more aware of their risk factors for heart disease and are taking steps to control them. If you also take such steps, you will improve your chances for living a long and healthy life. Remember, it is never too late. Changes you make at any time in your life to lessen your risk will make a difference.

It is important to know how to do CPR. The truth remains, however, that the best way to deal with cardiac arrest is to prevent it. If you go into cardiac arrest, your chances of surviving are poor. Waiting to deal with cardiac arrest after it happens is like placing an ambulance at the bottom of a 100-foot cliff to be there when you fall off. Once you fall off the cliff, it's unlikely that even the best care can save your life. Preventing cardiac arrest, on the other hand, is like placing a barrier at the top of the cliff to keep you from tumbling to your death. Begin to reduce your risk of heart disease today.

Preventing Heart Disease

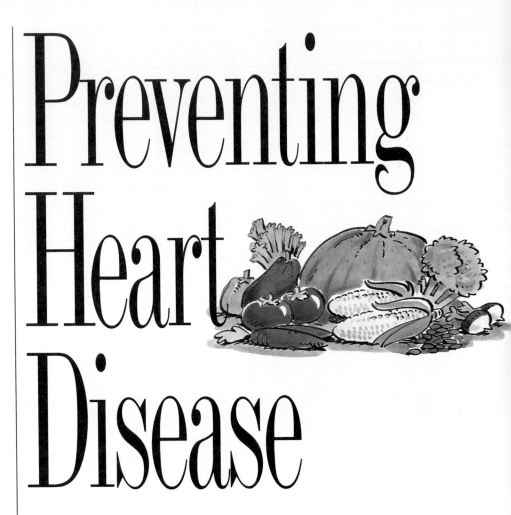

Heart disease is the leading cause of death for people over the age of 45 living in the United States. Although heart attacks may seem to strike suddenly, most of us make life-style choices every day that endanger our hearts. Over time, our choices can result in a heart attack or heart disease.

Scientists have identified factors that increase a person's chances of developing heart disease. These are known as risk factors. Some risk factors for heart disease cannot be changed. For example, men have a higher risk for heart disease than women. Having family members who have had heart disease also increases your risk.

Many risk factors for heart disease can be controlled. Smoking, diets high in fats, high blood pressure, obesity, and lack of routine exercise are all linked to increased risk of heart disease. When one risk factor, such as high blood pressure, is combined with other risk factors, the risk of heart attack or stroke is greatly increased. Managing your risk factors for heart disease really works. During the past 20 years, deaths from heart disease have gone down 33 percent in the United States, saving as many as 250,000 lives each year!

Smoking

Cigarette smokers have more than twice the chance of having a heart attack than non-smokers. They have two to four times the chance of cardiac arrest. The earlier a person starts smoking, the greater the risk to his or her health. Giving up smoking rapidly reduces the risk of heart disease. After a number of years, the risk for a person who stopped smoking is the same as the risk for a person who never smoked.

Recent studies indicate that even if you do not smoke, smoking may be increasing your risk of heart disease. Inhaling the smoke of others, called second-hand smoke, may be as dangerous as smoking. You should avoid long-term exposure to high levels of smoke and protect children from this potential danger. If you do not smoke, do not start. If you do smoke, quit.

Diet

Diets high in saturated fats and cholesterol increase the risk of heart disease. These diets raise the level of cholesterol found in the bloodstream. This increases the chances that cholesterol and other fatty deposits will be deposited on blood vessel walls, reducing blood flow.

Some cholesterol in the body is essential. The amount of cholesterol in the blood is determined by how much your body produces and by the food you eat. Foods high in cholesterol include egg yolks and organ meats such as liver, shrimp, and lobster.

A more significant contributor to an unhealthy blood-cholesterol level is saturated fat. Saturated fats raise the blood cholesterol level by interfering with the body's ability to remove cholesterol from the blood. Saturated fats are found in beef, lamb, veal, pork, ham, whole milk, and whole-milk products.

Rather than eliminating saturated fats and cholesterol from your diet, limit your intake. Moderation is the key. Make changes whenever possible. Substitute low fat or skimmed milk for whole milk and margarine for butter. Trim visible fat from meat and broil or bake instead of frying. Substitute fish for red meat occasionally. Eat fruit and vegetables for snacks instead of prepackaged or fast food. Read labels carefully. A "cholesterol free" product may actually be high in saturated fat.

Exercise

Routine exercise has many benefits, including increased muscle tone and weight control.

Exercise may also help you survive a heart attack because the increased circulation of blood through the heart develops additional channels for blood flow. If the primary channels that supply the heart are blocked in a heart attack, these additional channels can supply the heart with oxygen-rich blood.

Most of us wish we had more time to exercise. We know that exercise is good for almost every system in our body. But if you have limited time, it is best to build up cardiovascular fitness. Cardiovascular fitness can help you cope with stress, control your weight, ward off infections, improve self-esteem, sleep better, and accomplish your personal fitness goals.

To achieve cardiovascular fitness, you must exercise your heart. To do this, you should exercise at least three times a week for 20 to 30 minutes, maintaining your target heart rate range for at least 15 minutes. Your target heart rate range is 65 to 80 percent of your maximum heart rate. To find your target heart rate range, subtract your age from 220, then multiply that number by 0.65.

Consider a 40 year old who wants to exercise at 65 percent of his or her maximum heart rate. The target heart rate would be (220-40) x 0.65 = 117 beats per minute. This person should get his or her pulse rate to 117 beats per minute for at least 15 minutes during the workout.

As you exercise, take your pulse periodically at the wrist or neck. Exercise must be continuous and vigorous to maintain the target heart rate. As you build cardiovascular fitness, you will eventually be able to exercise for longer periods of time and at a higher target heart rate. The "no pain, no gain" theory is not a good approach to exercise. In fact, feeling pain usually means that you are exercising improperly. Be sure to warm up before vigorous exercise and cool down afterwards.

Turn your daily activities into exercise. Walk briskly or bicycle instead of driving. Climb the stairs instead of taking the elevator or escalator.

HEART HEALTHY IQ

The following statements represent a heart healthy life-style that can reduce your chances of heart disease. Check each statement that reflects your life-style.

- [ ] I do not smoke and I avoid inhaling the smoke of others.

- [ ] I eat a balanced diet that limits my intake of saturated fat and cholesterol.

- [ ] I participate in continuous, vigorous physical activity for 20 to 30 minutes or more at least three times a week.

- [ ] I have my blood pressure checked regularly.

- [ ] I maintain an appropriate weight.

If you did not check two or more of the statements, you should consider making changes in your life–style now.

Pedal an exercise bike or use a stair climber while watching TV, listening to music, or reading.

If you have not been exercising regularly or have health problems, see your doctor before starting an exercise program.

Blood Pressure

Uncontrolled high blood pressure can damage blood vessels in the heart and other organs. You can often control high blood pressure by losing excess weight and changing your diet. When these are not enough, a doctor can prescribe medications. You should take medications only as prescribed, and only your doctor should adjust them.

High blood pressure has no specific, easily recognized symptoms. It is important to have regular checkups to guard against high blood pressure and its effects. Free blood pressure checks may be available in your community at agencies, hospitals, health fairs, or pharmacies.

Weight

Many adults and children are overweight, some to the point of obesity. Obesity is defined as weighing 20 percent more than your desirable body weight. Obesity contributes to diseases such as heart disease, high blood pressure, diabetes, and gall bladder disease. However, body weight is not the main problem. The presence of too much body fat contributes to these diseases. See your doctor for help if you want a measure of your body fat.

Losing weight, especially fat, is no easy task. Weight loss and gain depend on a balance of intake of calories and output of energy. If you take in more calories than you use, you gain weight. If you use more calories that you take in, you lose weight.

Day-to-day weight changes reflect changes in the levels of fluids in your body. So if you are watching your weight, pick one day and time each week for your weigh-in. Track your weight loss based on this weekly amount, not on day-to-day differences.

Weight loss should always be combined with daily exercise. Any activity, such as walking to the bus, climbing the stairs, and cleaning the house, uses calories. The more active you are, the more calories you use.

Your eating habits should change as you grow older. If a person eats the same number of calories at the ages of 20 and 40 and maintains the same level of activity, he or she will be considerably heavier at 40 than at 20. It is important as you grow older to eat foods that provide your body with essential nutrients but are not high in calories.

When Seconds Count:

children

& Life-Threatening Emergencies

One in every 10 calls to your local EMS personnel is for an emergency involving children. If you are around children frequently, it is likely that you will have to care for a child or infant with an injury or illness. It is important to remember that children are not just small adults.

You might think that, because they are physically smaller, children do not need to breathe as fast as adults or that their hearts do not beat as fast.

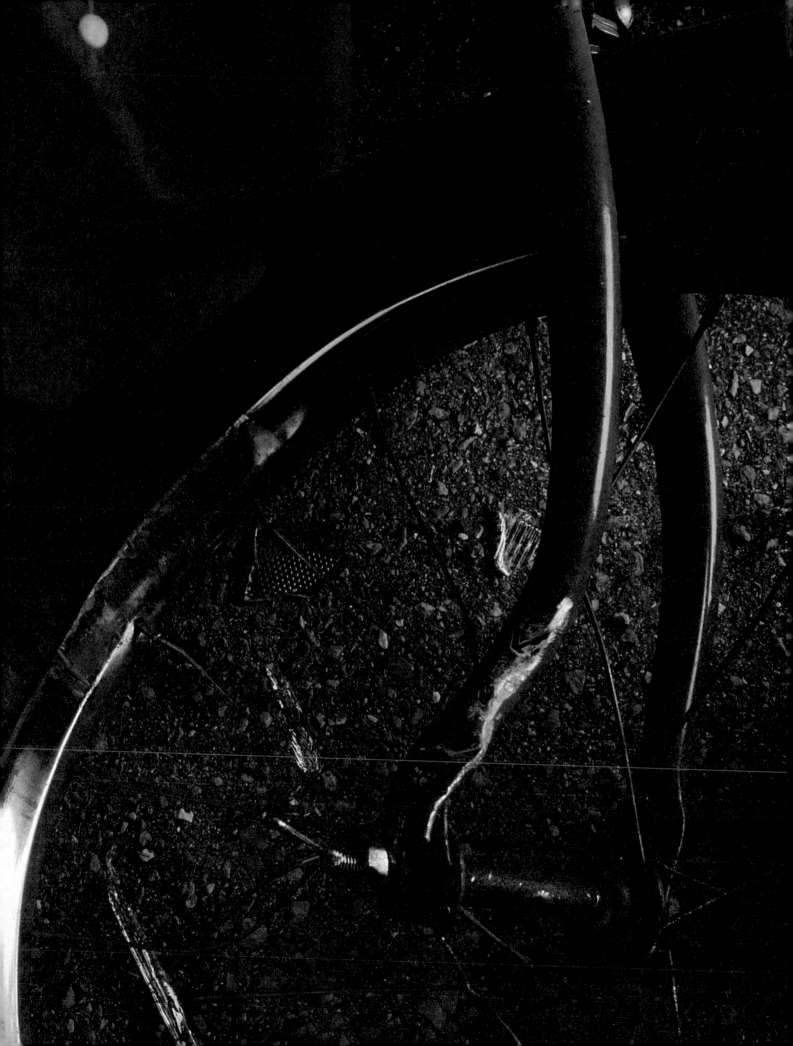

Injury...

is the leading cause of death of children in the U.S.

Children actually breathe faster than adults, and their hearts beat faster. The demands on their little bodies are great. In a breathing or cardiac emergency, children require care that is different from adults. Even among different-aged children, the care is somewhat different. Children from birth to 1 year of age receive slightly different care from that of children ages 1 to about 8.

In a life-threatening emergency, you must act at once. It may only be a matter of seconds before a child or infant dies. An emergency is life-threatening if the child or infant is unconscious, is not breathing, is breathing with difficulty, has no pulse, or is bleeding severely.

Let's take a look at the causes of life-threatening emergencies in children and infants. Before widespread immunization programs began about 40 years ago, infectious diseases, such as polio and diphtheria, were the main killers of chil-

dren. Now injury is the leading cause of death in children in the United States. The numbers are staggering. Every year 600,000 children are admitted to a hospital with injuries.

The six most common types of childhood injuries are motor vehicle passenger injuries, pedestrian injuries, bicycle injuries, drowning, burns, and firearm injuries (including unintentional injuries, homicides, and suicides).

Most injuries can be prevented. If they were, childhood deaths and disabilities would be greatly reduced. As children grow and develop and as they are exposed to different environments, they become vulnerable to different injuries and illnesses. Adults have the responsibility of making the environment safe for children. This can be done by—

- Keeping children away from things that might harm them.

Number of Children Killed in Accidents

Average Number Killed...

Total killed in 1989 = 7,860
(0 to 14 years of age)

Monthly Vital Statistics. Vol. 40, No. 8, Supplement 2. Jan. 7, 1992

Per Day

22

= 49 STUDENTS

Per Week

Per Month

151

Why KIDS Always Get Hurt

Children are naturally curious about people and objects in the world around them. They spend much of their time exploring and learning. At the same time, their small bodies are growing quickly and becoming more mobile. A child's developing body, however, is less skilled and more prone to injury than an adult's. A child's body proportions are also different from an adult's. For example, a child's head is quite large and heavy compared with the rest of the body. This puts children at greater risk for head injuries. Children's eyesight and hearing take time to fully develop. Thus they are often injured by traffic that they don't hear or see while walking or cycling.

One way infants learn about their world is by putting objects in their mouths. They also grasp and pull with their hands and wiggle and move their bodies. All of these actions can lead them into danger. The infant who can pick up a button or coin can put it in his or her mouth and choke. The infant who can pull a cup from a coffee table can be burned by hot liquid. The infant who can roll over can roll off a bed and suffer a head injury. Infants face many new dangers as they learn to roll, crawl, stand, climb, and walk. Infants cannot recognize dangers and it is up to adults to protect them. Often, protecting them is as simple as removing the dangers. A bottle of furniture polish stored

For more information on keeping children safe, contact:

Consumer Product Safety Commission
Washington, DC 20207
(800) 638-CPSC
Evaluates the safety of products sold to the public. Provides printed materials on consumer product safety topics on request.

National Maternal and Child Health Clearinghouse
8201 Greensboro Drive, Suite 600
McLean, VA 22102
(703) 821-8955, ext. 254
Provides information and printed materials on maternal and child health.

under a kitchen sink could poison a curious crawler. The danger can easily be removed by storing the polish in a locked cabinet where the child cannot reach it.

Like infants, toddlers and older children are always exploring and trying new things. Because they can walk, they tend to get into more trouble than infants do. They learn to copy adult behaviors and begin to understand how things work. They use words to ask for things and talk to other people, yet they lack judgment and understanding of potential risks. For instance, children cannot judge the depth of water.

Children are often injured when they are left alone, even for a few minutes. Young children need constant adult guidance and supervision, but the amount and kind of supervision needed changes as children grow and develop.

You can teach children safety in two ways. First, you can set an example of safe behavior by acting safely yourself. Second, you can encourage children to act safely by giving them simple, clear instructions about what they should and should not do. For example, teach children to always buckle their safety belts. Explain to them how a safety belt protects them from getting hurt. Teach them that they should not touch a hot stove and explain the meaning of the word *hot*. Remember to be patient. It takes time to learn safe behaviors and make them a habit.

GENERAL SAFETY RULES

Here are some basic safety rules you can follow to protect children:

Buckle up children in motor vehicles.

Always watch children in or near water.

Never keep loaded guns in your home.

Use gates on stairs.

Keep plastic bags, cords, and small objects away from young children.

Call the Poison Control Center if you think a child has been poisoned.

Have a plan for dealing with emergencies.

Check your home for fire and burn dangers.

- Staying near children so you can act in case of an emergency.
- Following safety rules yourself and teaching them to children.

Breathing Emergencies

The human body needs a constant supply of oxygen to stay alive. During breathing, air enters the nose and mouth. The air travels down the throat, through the windpipe, and into the lungs. This pathway from the nose and mouth to the lungs is called the airway. As you might well imagine, a child's airway is much smaller than an adult's. But as for an adult, the airway must be open for air to go into the lungs. In the lungs the oxygen in the air is picked up by the blood. The heart pumps the blood through the body. The blood flows through the blood vessels, taking the oxygen to the brain and to all other parts of the body.

A breathing emergency happens when air cannot travel freely and easily into the lungs. Some emergencies are life-threatening because they greatly cut down on the oxygen the body needs or cut off the oxygen entirely. For example, the body's supply of oxygen may be cut down when someone has difficulty breathing. However, when breathing stops, the oxygen supply is completely cut off. The heart will soon stop beating and blood will no longer move through the body. Unless the brain gets oxygen within minutes, brain damage or death will occur.

A breathing problem so severe that it threatens the victim's life is a breathing emergency. It is very im-

portant to recognize breathing emergencies in children and infants and to act before the heart stops beating. This is often the key to saving a child or infant's life.

Adult hearts frequently stop beating because they are diseased. For example, heart attacks are a common result of heart disease. Children's hearts, however, are usually healthy. When a child's heart stops, it is usually the result of a breathing emergency. If the child cannot breathe properly, not enough oxygen gets into the blood. This starves the heart of oxygen, and the heart soon stops beating. Children whose hearts stop beating rarely survive. Of the few who do most suffer permanent brain damage.

Most cardiac emergencies in children can be prevented. There are three main ways to do this. One way is to keep children from being injured. A second is to make sure children have proper medical care. A third is to learn to recognize the early signals of a breathing emergency and what to do about such an emergency.

Breathing emergencies can be caused by injury or illness. Injury or disease in areas of the brain that control breathing can disturb or stop breathing. A major cause of breathing emergencies is choking on a piece of food or a small object.

Damage to the muscles or bones of the chest can make breathing painful or difficult. Electric shock and drowning can cause

Adults are responsible... for making sure children are safe.

Air travels to the lungs by way of the airway, where oxygen is transferred to the blood. Oxygen-rich blood is transported to the brain, heart, and other parts of the body.

O_2 O_2 O_2 O_2 O_2 O_2 O_2 O_2 O_2

655

breathing to stop. Allergic reactions may make the airway swell shut. Reactions to poisons, anxiety, excitement, and conditions such as asthma can all cause breathing emergencies.

Asthma is a condition that narrows the air passages and makes breathing difficult. It may be triggered by an allergic reaction to food, pollen, medications, bites, or stings or by physical or emotional stress. A typical signal of asthma is wheezing when the child breathes out. A child's chest may look larger than normal because air becomes trapped in the lungs. Normally, asthma is controlled with medication. Medications open the airway and make breathing easier.

Hyperventilation occurs when a child breathes faster than normal. Causes include fear, or anxiety, injuries, illnesses such as high fever, and diabetic emergencies. It can also result from asthma or exercise. A typical signal of hyperventilation is shallow, rapid breathing. Despite trying hard to breathe, children who are hyperventilating say they

Unless the brain gets oxygen...

brain damage or death will occur within minutes.

SIGNALS OF A BREATHING EMERGENCY

CHECK BREATHING
Breathing is —
Slower or faster than usual.
Noisy.
Painful.

Child or infant is —
Gasping for breath.
Wheezing, gurgling, or making high-pitched sounds.

CHECK SKIN
Skin is more moist than usual.
Skin looks flushed, pale, or bluish.

ASK HOW CHILD FEELS
Child feels —
Short of breath.
Dizzy or light-headed.
Pain in the chest.
Tingling in the hands and feet.

If you see any signals of a breathing emergency, you should get medical care at once!

cannot get enough air or that they are suffocating. Therefore they are often frightened and confused. They may say that they feel dizzy or that their fingers and toes feel numb or tingly.

A severe allergic reaction can cause the airway to swell and restrict breathing. It may result from insect stings, food, or medications, such as penicillin. If you know a child is allergic to certain substances, keep the child away from them. A physician may recommend that the child or an adult guardian carry medication to reverse the reaction.

Signals of allergic reaction may develop very quickly. They include a rash, a feeling of tightness in the chest and throat, and swelling of the face, neck, and tongue. The child may feel dizzy or confused. If not cared for at once, severe allergic reactions can become life-threatening.

Even though there are many causes of breathing emergencies, you don't have to know the exact cause to respond. You do need to be able to recognize the signals of a breathing emergency and take action fast!

Recognizing Breathing Emergencies

You are most likely to have to care for a conscious child or infant who is having difficulty breathing. You will probably be able to identify a breathing problem by watching and listening to the way the child or infant breathes. A child who can talk may be able to tell you what is wrong.

Normal breathing is easy and quiet. Children should not have to work at breathing. Breaths should be regular, and breathing should not be painful.

When a child's heart stops...

it is usually the result of a breathing emergency.

There are many signals of breathing emergencies. They might not be the same for all children. Children and infants may look as if they can't catch their breath, or they may gasp for air. They may be breathing faster or slower than normal. Their breaths may be deeper or more shallow than usual. They may make unusual noises, such as wheezing or gurgling, or high-pitched sounds.

The child's skin may also signal that something is wrong. At first, the child's skin may be more moist than usual and look flushed. Later, it may look pale or bluish as the oxygen level in the blood falls.

A child having a breathing problem may feel dizzy or light-headed. The child may complain that his or her chest hurts and that his or her hands and feet are tingling. The child may be frightened.

Any of these signals indicates a breathing emergency. In short, any breathing that is noisy, painful, or unusually fast or slow is a breathing emergency.

A child who can talk may be able to tell you that he or she finds it difficult to breathe. For infants and very young children, though, you must use your own judgment based on how the child looks and the way he or she is breathing. If you see any signals of a breathing emergency, you should get medical care at once.

Make Your Home Safe for Kids

Storage Areas

YES/NO Are pesticides, detergents, and other household chemicals kept out of child's reach?

YES/NO Are tools kept out of child's reach?

General Safety Precautions Inside the Home

YES/NO Are stairways kept clear and uncluttered?

YES/NO Are stairs and hallways well lit?

YES/NO Are safety gates installed at tops and bottoms of stairways?

YES/NO Are guards installed around fireplaces, radiators or hot pipes, and wood-burning stoves?

YES/NO Are sharp edges of furniture cushioned with corner guards or other material?

YES/NO Are unused electric outlets covered with tape or safety covers?

YES/NO Are curtain cords and shade pulls kept out of child's reach?

YES/NO Are windows secured with window locks?

YES/NO Are plastic bags kept out of child's reach?

YES/NO Are fire extinguishers installed where they are most likely to be needed?

YES/NO Are smoke detectors in working order?

YES/NO Do you have an emergency plan to use in case of fire? Does your family practice this plan?

YES/NO Is the water set at a safe temperature? (A setting of 120° F or less prevents scalding from tap water in sinks and in tubs. Let the water run for three minutes before testing it.)

YES/NO If you have a gun, is it locked in a place where your child cannot get it?

YES/NO Are all purses, handbags, brief cases, and so on, including those of visitors, kept out of child's reach?

YES/NO Are all poisonous plants kept out of child's reach?

YES/NO Is a list of emergency phone numbers posted near a telephone?

YES/NO Is a list of instructions posted near a telephone for use by children and/or babysitters?

Bathroom

YES/NO Are the toilet seat and lid kept down when the toilet is not in use?

YES/NO Are cabinets equipped with safety latches and kept closed?

YES/NO Are all medicines in child-resistant containers and stored in a locked medicine cabinet?

YES/NO Are shampoos and cosmetics stored out of child's reach?

YES/NO Are razors, razor blades, and other sharp objects kept out of child's reach?

YES/NO Are hair dryers and other appliances stored away from sink, tub, and toilet?

YES/NO Does the bottom of tub or shower have rubber stickers or a rubber mat to prevent slipping?

YES/NO Is the child always watched by an adult while in the tub?

Kitchen

YES/NO	Do you cook on back stove burners when possible and turn pot handles toward the back of the stove?
YES/NO	Are hot dishes kept away from the edges of tables and counters?
YES/NO	Are hot liquids and foods kept out of child's reach?
YES/NO	Are knives and other sharp items kept out of child's reach?
YES/NO	Is the highchair placed away from stove and other hot appliances?
YES/NO	Are matches and lighters kept out of child's reach?
YES/NO	Are all appliance cords kept out of child's reach?
YES/NO	Are cabinets equipped with safety latches?
YES/NO	Are cabinet doors kept closed when not in use?
YES/NO	Are cleaning products kept out of child's reach?
YES/NO	Do you test the temperature of heated food before feeding the child?

Use this checklist to spot dangers in your home. When you read each question, circle either the "Yes" box or the "No" box. Each "No" shows a possible danger for you and your family. Work with your family to remove dangers and make your home safer.

Child's Room

YES/NO	Is child's bed or crib placed away from radiators and other hot surfaces?
YES/NO	Are crib slats no more than 2-3/8 inches apart?
YES/NO	Does the mattress fit the sides of the crib snugly?
YES/NO	Is paint or finish on furniture and toys nontoxic?
YES/NO	Are electric cords kept out of child's reach?
YES/NO	Is the child's clothing, especially sleepwear, flame resistant?
YES/NO	Does the toy box have a secure lid and safe-closing hinges?
YES/NO	Are the toys in good repair?
YES/NO	Are toys appropriate for the child's age?

Outside the Home/Play Areas

YES/NO	Is trash kept in tightly covered containers?
YES/NO	Are walkways, stairs, and railings in good repair?
YES/NO	Are walkways and stairs free of toys, tools, and other objects?
YES/NO	Are sandboxes and wading pools covered when not in use?
YES/NO	Are swimming pools nearby enclosed with a fence that your child cannot easily climb over?
YES/NO	Is playground equipment safe? Is it assembled according to the manufacturer's instructions and anchored over a level, soft surface such as sand or wood chips?

Parents Bedroom

YES/NO	Are space heaters kept away from curtains and flammable materials?
YES/NO	Are cosmetics, perfumes, and breakable items stored out of child's reach?
YES/NO	Are small objects, such as jewelry, buttons, and safety pins, kept out of child's reach?

CHILD SAFETY IQ

- [ ] Do you buckle your child into an approved automobile safety seat even when making short trips?
- [ ] Do you teach your child safety by behaving safely in your own everyday activities?
- [ ] Do you supervise your child whenever he or she is around water and maintain fences and gates that act as barriers to water?
- [ ] Have you checked your home for potential fire hazards? Are smoke detectors installed and working?
- [ ] Are all poisonous substances — cleaning supplies, medicines, plants, etc.— kept out of a child's reach?
- [ ] Are foods and small items that can choke a child kept out of reach?
- [ ] Have you inspected your home, day-care center, school, babysitter's home, or wherever your child spends time for potential safety and health hazards?
- [ ] Do you keep guns and ammunition stored separately and locked up?

CARING FOR

BREAT

EMERG

CHILDREN WITH

THING

ENCIES

Recognizing the signals of breathing emergencies and caring for them are often keys to preventing other emergencies. A breathing problem may signal the beginning of a life-threatening condition.

IF A CHILD OR INFANT HAS TROUBLE BREATHING

If a conscious child or infant is having trouble breathing, help him or her rest in a comfortable position. Sitting usually makes breathing easier. Make sure someone has called the local emergency number for help. Stay with the child or infant until an ambulance arrives.

Remember that children who are having difficulty breathing may have trouble talking. Talk to any bystanders who may know the child's problem. Children often answer yes-or-no questions by nodding. Keep checking breathing and skin appearance. Try to reduce any anxiety that might have contributed to the breathing problem by comfort-

If a conscious infant or child is having trouble breathing, support him or her in a sitting position.

Care for an infant is slightly different than for a child.

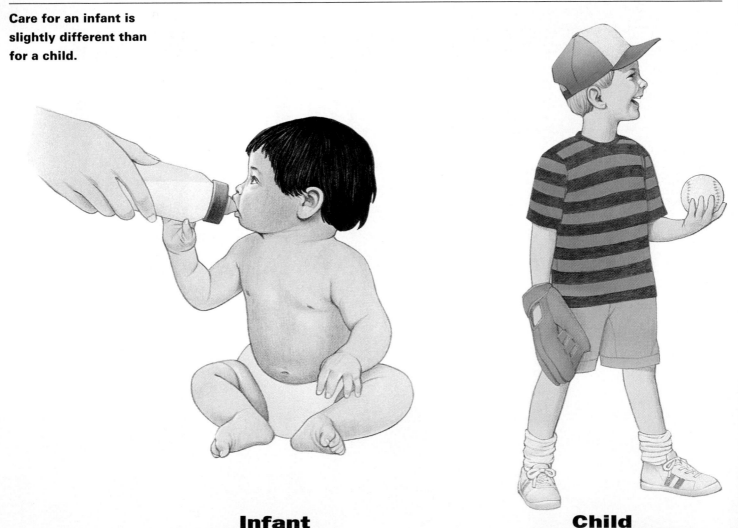

**Infant
(0-1 YEAR)**

**Child
(1-8 YEARS)**

ing him or her. Help keep the child or infant from getting chilled or overheated. Help give any medication prescribed for a particular condition.

If the child or infant is breathing rapidly (hyperventilating) and you are sure it is caused by emotion, such as excitement, not injury or illness, try to get the child to relax and breathe slowly. Reassurance is often enough to correct hyperventilation. If the child's breathing still does not return to normal or if the child becomes unconscious from hyperventilating, call the local emergency number right away.

If you recognize the signals of a breathing emergency and can provide care, you may be able to prevent the condition from developing into a more serious emergency. If the child stops breathing, he or she may die without immediate care.

The care for infants and for children with breathing emergencies is similar. But as you read earlier, some of the techniques are a little different because infants and children vary in size. In general, skills that are described for a child should be used for a child from about age 1 to about age 8. Infant skills should be used for those under 1 year of age. A general guideline is to perform infant skills on a child or infant about the length of your thigh or whom you can comfortably support with your forearm and hand. Perform child skills on a child who is larger than this.

CARING FOR BREATHING DIFFICULTY

Call the local emergency phone number for help.

Help the child or infant rest in the position easiest for breathing.

Comfort the child or infant.

Keep checking breathing.

Make sure the child or infant does not get chilled or overheated.

Give any prescribed medication.

PREVENTING CHOKING

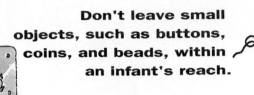

Don't leave small objects, such as buttons, coins, and beads, within an infant's reach.

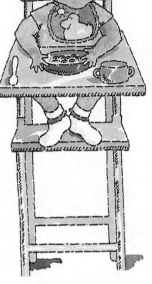

Have children sit in a high chair or at a table while they eat.

Do not let children eat too fast.

Give infants soft food that they do not need to chew.

Make sure that toys are too large to be swallowed.

Do not give infants and young children foods like nuts, grapes, popcorn, and raw vegetables.

Make sure that toys have no small parts that could be pulled off.

Cut foods a child can choke on easily, such as hot dogs, into small pieces.

Supervise children while they eat.

IF A CHILD IS CHOKING

Choking is a common childhood injury that can lead to death. When a child is choking, the airway is partly or completely blocked, usually by food or other small objects. Children often choke while they are eating and can choke on a very small piece of food. Also, children cannot or do not always chew food well. Some foods that an adult can eat easily can cause a child to choke.

Tasting is one way children explore their world. Young children, especially those under the age of three, often put objects, such as coins, beads, and toys, in their mouths. This is normal, but it can lead to choking.

A choking child can quickly stop breathing, lose consciousness, and die. Therefore it is very impor-

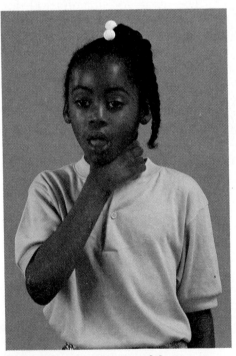

Clutching the throat with one or both hands is universally recognized as a distress signal for choking.

Encourage a choking child who is coughing forcefully to continue coughing.

tant to recognize when a child needs first aid for choking. One of the signals of choking is coughing. Sometimes a child who is choking will cough forcefully. At other times the child may cough weakly or make a high-pitched sound while coughing. A child who is not able to breathe or cough at all may panic and clutch his or her throat with one or both hands.

If the child is coughing forcefully, the airway is partially blocked but the child is still able to get some air. Stay with the child. Tell the child to keep on coughing. The coughing may clear the airway. If the child does not stop coughing soon or docs not cough up the object, call the local emergency number for help.

If the child is coughing weakly or is making a high-pitched sound or if the child cannot speak, breathe, or cough, the airway is completely blocked. You must give first aid right away. Try to remove the object that is blocking the airway by creating an artificial cough. Wrap your arms around the child's waist. Make a fist with one hand and place it against the middle of the child's abdomen, just above the navel. Grab your fist with your other hand. Give quick upward thrusts into the abdomen until the object is forced out.

Stop giving thrusts as soon as the child coughs up the object or

If a child is choking, give quick, upward thrusts to the abdomen, just above the navel, until the object is forced out.

If Child is Unable to Speak, Cough, or Breathe...

starts to breathe or cough. Watch the child and make sure that he or she is breathing freely again. Even after the child coughs up the object, the child may have breathing problems that will need a doctor's attention. Also, abdominal thrusts may cause injuries. For these reasons, you should call the local emergency number if you have not already done so. The child should be taken to the hospital emergency department to be checked by a physician. Do this even if the child seems to be breathing well.

SKILL SHEET

STEP 1

Place thumb side of fist against middle of abdomen just above the navel. Grasp fist with other hand.

STEP 2

Give quick upward thrusts.

Repeat until object is coughed up or child becomes unconscious.

IF A CHILD IS NOT BREATHING

A child may stop breathing because of illness, injury, or a blocked airway. A child who is not breathing gets no oxygen. The body can function only for a few minutes without oxygen before body systems begin to fail.

A child who is not breathing needs rescue breathing. Rescue breathing is a way of breathing air into a person to supply the oxygen he or she needs to survive. Rescue breathing is given to any child who is not breathing.

You discover whether you need to give rescue breathing when you check an unconscious child. If the child is not breathing but has a pulse, begin rescue breathing. Begin by tilting the head back and lifting the chin to move the tongue away from the back of the throat.

This opens the airway. Place your ear next to the child's mouth. Look, listen, and feel for breathing for about 5 seconds. If you can't see, hear, or feel any signs of breathing, pinch the child's nose shut and make a tight seal around the child's mouth with your mouth. Breathe slowly into the child until you see the chest rise. Do this two times. Each breath should last about 1½ seconds. Pause between each breath to let the air flow back out. Watch the child's chest rise each time you breathe into the child to be sure that your breaths are actually going in.

Check for a pulse at the side of the neck. If a pulse is present but the child is still not breathing, give one breath about every 3 seconds. A good way to time the breaths is to count "one one-thousand, take a breath on "two-one-thousand" and

1 BREATH

4

3 SECONDS

If there is a pulse but the child is not breathing, give one breath about every 3 seconds.

If someone is with you when you discover an unconscious child, have that person phone for help while you continue to give care.

If a child stops breathing, you must breathe for him or her. This is called rescue breathing.

1 MINUTE

If you are alone and the child is not breathing, give rescue breathing for about 1 minute before calling your emergency number.

breathe into the child on "three one-thousand."

After about 1 minute of rescue breathing (about 20 breaths), re-check the pulse. If the child still has a pulse but is not breathing, continue rescue breathing. Check the pulse every minute. Continue rescue breathing until one of the following happens:

- The child begins to breathe on his or her own.
- The child has no pulse (begin CPR).
- Another trained rescuer takes over for you.
- You are too tired to go on.

Call the local emergency number for help if a child is unconscious. If someone is with you when you discover an unconscious child, have that person phone for help immediately. This way, you can continue checking the child and give rescue breathing or any other necessary care at once. If you are alone and you find a child unconscious and not breathing, give rescue breathing for about 1 minute before calling the local emergency number. This delay in phoning allows you to give breaths that will get oxygen into the child and prevent the heart from stopping. If the child is small enough, carry him or her to the telephone while continuing to give breaths.

When you are giving rescue breathing, you want to avoid getting air in the child's stomach instead of the lungs. This may happen if you breathe into the child too long, breathe too hard, or don't open the airway far enough.

To avoid getting air in the child's stomach, keep the child's head tilted back. Breathe *slowly* into the child, just enough to make the chest rise. Each breath should last about 1½ seconds. Pause between breaths long enough for the air in the child's lungs to come out and for you to take another breath.

If the child is small enough, carry him or her to the phone while you continue to give breaths.

If vomiting occurs, turn the child on his or her side and wipe the mouth clean.

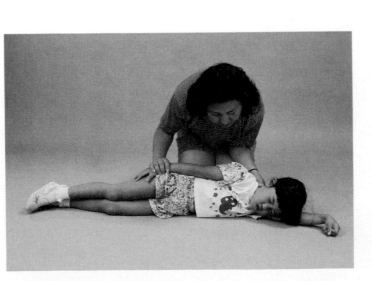

Air in the stomach can make the child vomit. When an unconscious child vomits, the contents of the stomach can get into the lungs and block breathing. Air in the stomach also makes it harder for the diaphragm, the large muscle that controls breathing, to move. This makes it harder for the lungs to fill with air.

Even when you are giving rescue breathing properly, the child may vomit. If this happens, roll the child onto one side and wipe the mouth clean. If possible, use latex

For mouth-to-nose breathing, close the child's mouth, seal your mouth around the child's nose, and breathe into the nose.

gloves, gauze, or even a handkerchief when you sweep out the mouth. Then roll the child on his or her back again and continue with rescue breathing.

Sometimes you might not be able to make a tight enough seal over a child's mouth. For example, the child's jaw or mouth may be injured or shut too tightly to open. If you can't make a tight seal over the mouth, you can breathe into the nose. With the head tilted backward, close the child's mouth by gently pushing on the chin. Seal your mouth around the child's nose and breathe into the nose. If possible, open the child's mouth between breaths to let the air out.

Finally, you should suspect head, neck, or back injuries if a child has fallen from a height or has been in a motor vehicle crash. If you suspect such an injury, try not to move the child's head and neck. If you need to open the airway, do so by lifting the child's chin without tilting the head back. This may be enough to allow air to pass into the lungs. If you try to give breaths and your breaths are not going in, you should tilt the head back very slightly. This will usually allow air to pass into the lungs. If air still does not go in, tilt the head farther back. It is unlikely that this action will make any injuries worse. Remember that if a child isn't breathing, his or her greatest need is for air.

SKILL SHEET

If Child is Not Breathing...

If you suspect a head or spine injury, try to open the airway by lifting the chin without tilting the head.

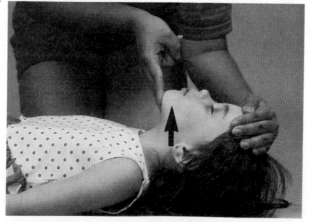

Give Rescue Breathing

STEP 1
With head tilted back, pinch the nose shut.

STEP 2
Give 2 slow breaths. Breathe in until chest gently rises.

STEP 3
Check for a pulse.

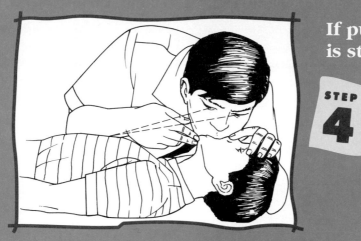

If pulse is present but child is still not breathing ...

STEP 4 Give 1 slow breath about every 3 seconds. Do this for about 1 minute (15 breaths).

STEP 5 Recheck pulse and breathing about every minute.

Call the local emergency number if you have not already done so. Then, continue rescue breathing as long as pulse is present but person is not breathing.

Recheck pulse about every minute.

IF AIR WON'T GO IN

You may find that an unconscious child's chest does not rise and fall as you give breaths. If you did not tilt the head back far enough, the child's tongue may be blocking the throat. Retilt the child's head and give two more breaths. If you still cannot breathe air into the child, the child's airway is probably blocked. The airway can be blocked by food, a small object such as a toy or coin, or fluids such as blood and saliva. Tell someone to phone the local emergency number for help while you provide care.

The most important thing to do is to try to remove the object or move it enough so you can get air past it into the lungs. First, try to create an artificial cough to force air—and the object—out of the airway. To do this, press both hands into the child's abdomen with quick upward thrusts. To give thrusts, straddle the child. Place the heel of one hand on the middle of the abdomen just above the navel. Place the other hand on top of the first. Give thrusts toward the head. Give up to five thrusts, then look to see if the object is in the child's mouth. If you can see the object, slide a finger down the inside of the child's cheek and try to hook the object out. Next give two breaths.

If your first attempts to clear the airway don't succeed, repeat the abdominal thrusts, object checks, and breaths. The longer the child goes without oxygen, the more the muscles of the throat will relax. This will make it more likely you will be able to remove the object or breathe past it.

If you do clear the airway and can breathe into the child, give two slow breaths and check the child's pulse. If there is a pulse, check for breathing. If the child is not breathing on his or her own, continue rescue breathing.

If the child starts breathing on his or her own, keep the airway open and continue to check breathing until EMS personnel arrive and take over.

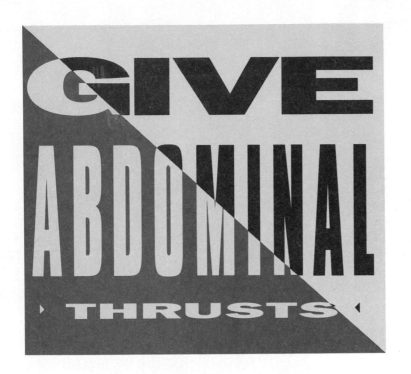

If you are unable to breathe air into the child, the airway is probably blocked. Give abdominal thrusts.

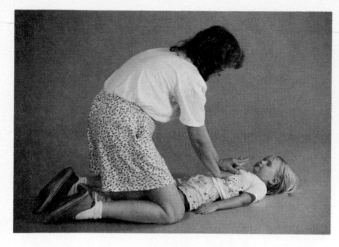

To give abdominal thrusts to a child, straddle the legs, position your hands with your fingers pointing toward the victim's head and give quick, upward thrusts.

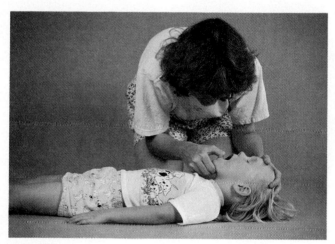

Look for an object in the throat. Slide a finger down inside of the cheek and try to hook the object out only if you can see it.

SKILL SHEET

If Air Does Not Go In...

Open the airway and attempt to give two breaths.

Give Abdominal Thrusts

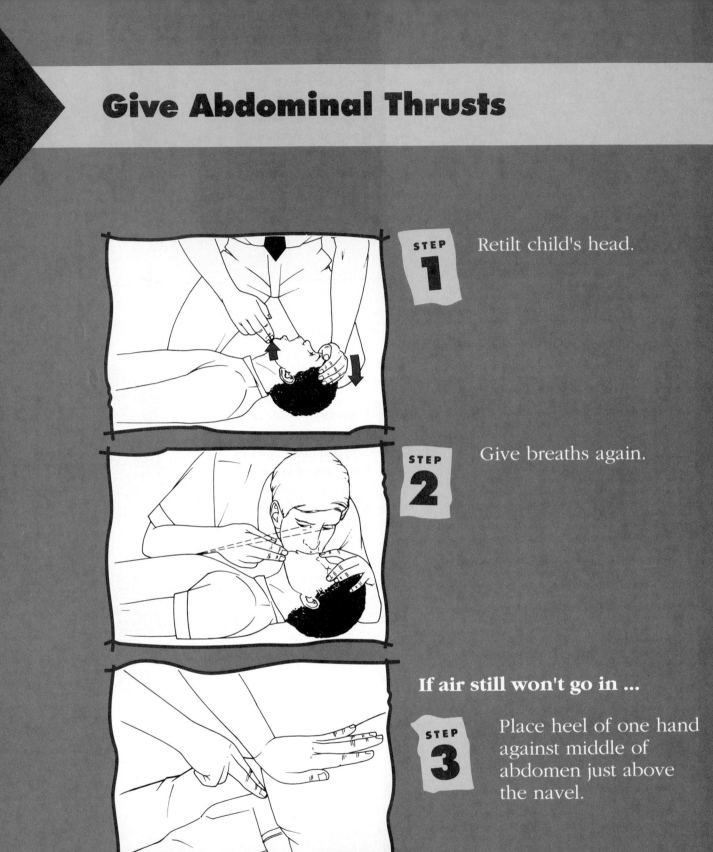

STEP 1 — Retilt child's head.

STEP 2 — Give breaths again.

If air still won't go in ...

STEP 3 — Place heel of one hand against middle of abdomen just above the navel.

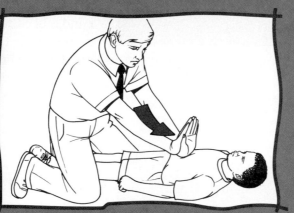

 STEP 4

Give up to 5 abdominal thrusts.

STEP 5

Lift jaw and tongue and check for object. If seen, sweep it out with finger.

STEP 6

Tilt head back and give breaths again.

Repeat breaths, thrusts, and sweeps until breaths go in or child starts to breathe on own.

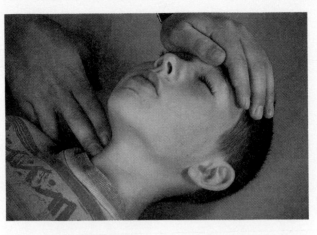

For a child, check for a pulse at the side of the neck.

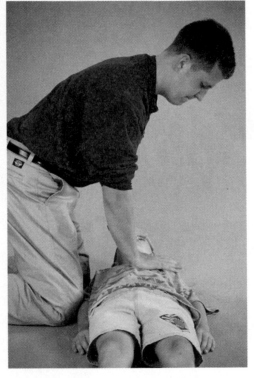

To give compressions, keep the head tilted back and place the heel of your other hand on the lower half of the breastbone. Press the chest down and then release it in a smooth, even rhythm.

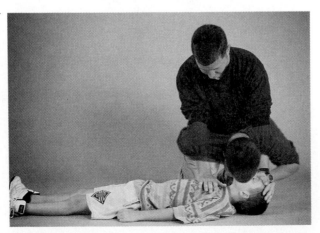

When giving CPR, alternate chest compressions and rescue breathing.

IF THE CHILD DOES NOT HAVE A PULSE

Your check of an unconscious child includes checking breathing and pulse. If the child is not breathing, it is likely that his or her heart will stop beating. Checking the pulse can tell you whether or not the child's heart has stopped. For a child, check for a pulse at the side of the neck. If you can't feel the pulse after checking for about 5 to 10 seconds, you should start cardiopulmonary resuscitation (CPR).

CPR has two parts. One part is chest compressions. When you give chest compressions, press down and let up on the lower half of the breastbone. The second part of CPR is rescue breathing. When you give CPR, alternate chest compressions and rescue breathing.

When you breathe into the lungs of a child who has stopped breathing, you keep the lungs supplied with oxygen. The oxygen in the lungs goes into the blood. When you compress the chest, you keep blood flowing through the child's body. The blood carries oxygen to the brain, heart, and other parts of the body. CPR keeps oxygen-carrying blood flowing through the body, especially to the brain.

You must start CPR as soon as possible after the child's heart stops beating. If brain cells don't get oxygen, they begin to die after 4 minutes. Starting CPR right away increases the chances that the child will survive.

Once you have decided that the child needs CPR, you must put yourself and the child in the correct position. Place the child on his or her back, on a firm, level surface. Kneel beside the child's chest. Keep the child's head tilted back with one hand. Place your other

5 COMPRESSIONS **1 BREATH**

If the child is not breathing and has no pulse, give cycles of five compressions and one breath.

hand on the breastbone in the middle of the child's chest and then push down and let up five times. Each compression should be about 1½ inches deep. These 5 compressions should take about 3 seconds. Count, "one, two, three, . . ." to help you maintain an even and regular rhythm.

After giving 5 compressions, you must get oxygen into the child's lungs. With the head tilted back, lift the chin, and give 1 slow breath (for about 1½ seconds) until the chest rises. Continue this cycle of 5 compressions and 1 breath. Do about 12 cycles of CPR (about one minute). Then recheck the pulse. If you can't feel the pulse, continue CPR until help arrives. Recheck every few minutes for pulse and breathing.

If Child is Not Breathing and Has No Pulse...

Give CPR

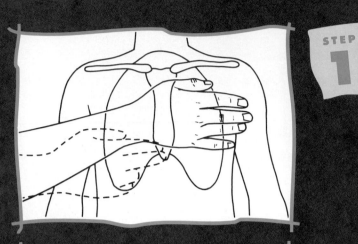

STEP 1 Find hand position on about the center of the breastbone.

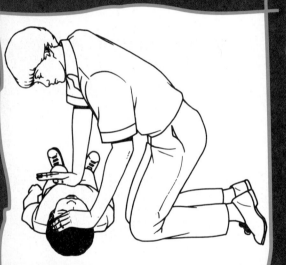

STEP 2 Position shoulders over hands. Compress chest 5 times.

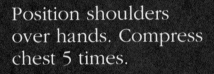

STEP 3 Give 1 slow breath.

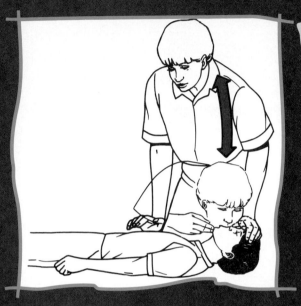

STEP 4

Repeat cycles of 5 compressions and 1 breath for about 1 minute (about 12 cycles).

Call the local emergency number if you have not already done so. Then...

STEP 5

Recheck pulse and breathing for about 5 seconds.

If there is still no pulse ...

STEP 6

Continue sets of 5 compressions and 1 breath. Recheck pulse and breathing every few minutes.

Caring for *Infants* With Breathing Emergencies

It was noted in the previous article that the care for infants (birth to 1 year) and children with breathing and cardiac emergencies is similar. Care differs in a few areas because infants and children vary in size. In general the skills presented here should be used for an infant under 1 year of age. If you are uncertain of the infant's age, use your own judgment. If an infant is too long or too heavy for you to support him or her on your arm and hand, especially if the infant is choking, use the technique for a child.

REMINDER:

Infants can easily choke on such foods as nuts, grapes, and popcorn.

If an Infant is Choking

Choking is a major cause of death and injury in infants. One reason is that infants learn about their world by putting objects in their mouths. Small objects, such as pebbles, coins, beads, and parts of toys, are dangerous if an infant puts them in the mouth. Infants also often choke because it takes a long time to develop their eating skills. Infants can easily choke on some foods that an adult can eat, such as nuts, grapes, or popcorn.

To prevent choking, never let an infant eat alone. Never prop up a bottle for an infant to drink alone.

Always stay with an infant during meals or snacks. Cut food into small pieces. Do not give an infant foods, such as nuts, that could lodge in the airway. If you suspect that an infant has an object in his or her mouth, check with your fingers and remove it. Regularly check floors, rugs, and other places for pins, coins, and other small objects that an infant might pick up and put in his or her mouth.

Like a child who is choking, a choking infant can quickly stop breathing, lose consciousness, and die. If the infant is coughing forcefully, allow the infant to continue to cough. Watch the infant carefully. If the infant does not stop coughing in a few minutes or if the infant coughs weakly, makes a high-pitched sound while coughing, or cannot cry, cough, or breathe, have someone call the local emergency number for help. To clear a blocked airway, you will need to give back blows and chest thrusts.

To do this, position the infant facedown on your arm, with your hand supporting the infant's head. With your other hand, strike the infant between the shoulder blades 5 times. Turn the infant over, place two or three fingers in the center of the breast bone, and give 5 chest thrusts. Each thrust should be about 1 inch deep. Turn the infant facedown again and repeat back blows, followed by chest thrusts.

Stop as soon as the object is coughed up or the infant starts to breathe or cough. Watch the infant and make sure that he or she is breathing freely again. Call the local emergency number if you have not already done so. The infant should be taken to the hospital emergency department to be checked by a doctor. Do this even if the infant seems to be breathing well.

To clear a blocked airway, you will need to repeat a series of 5 back blows and 5 chest thrusts.

BACK 5 BLOWS · CHEST 5 THRUSTS

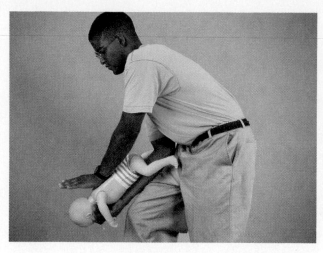

Position the infant facedown on your forearm so that the head is lower than the chest. Give 5 back blows between the shoulder blades (*top*). Turn the infant onto his or her back (*middle*). Give 5 chest thrusts in the center of the breastbone (*bottom*).

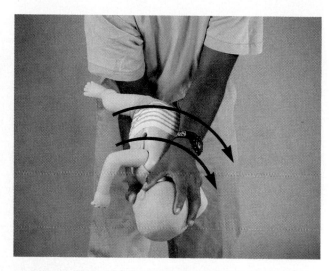

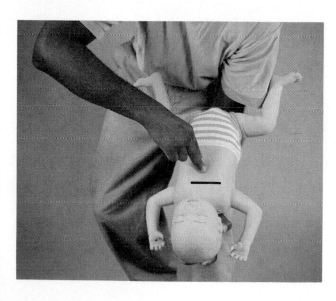

If Infant is Unable to Cry, Cough, or Breathe...

Give Back Blows and Chest Thrusts

STEP 1

With infant facedown on forearm, give 5 back blows with heel of hand between infant's shoulder blades.

STEP 2

Position infant faceup on forearm.

STEP 3

Give 5 chest thrusts on about the center of the breastbone.

Repeat back blows and chest thrusts until object is coughed up, infant begins to breathe on own, or infant becomes unconcious.

An infant who is not breathing needs rescue breathing. Give 1 breath about every 3 seconds.

If an Infant is Not Breathing

When an infant stops breathing, his or her body can function for only for a few minutes without oxygen before body systems begin to fail. Like a child, an infant who is not breathing but has a pulse needs rescue breathing immediately. Rescue breathing provides the oxygen the infant needs to survive. You discover whether you need to give rescue breathing when you check the infant's breathing and pulse. You do not need to tip an infant's head back very far to open the airway. You will know the airway is open if you can see the infant's chest rise and fall as you give breaths.

Because an infant's mouth is so small, you should seal your mouth over the infant's mouth and nose instead of just over the mouth as you would for a child. Breathe slowly into the infant only until you see the chest rise. Each breath should last about 1 to 1½ seconds. Pause in between breaths to let the air flow back out. Watch the chest rise each time you breathe in to be sure that your breaths are actually going in. Give 1 breath about every 3 seconds. A good way to time the breaths is to count "one one-thousand," take a breath yourself on "two one-thousand," and breathe into the infant on "three one-thousand." Remember to breathe slowly and gently. Breathing too hard or too fast can force air into the infant's stomach.

After 1 minute of rescue breathing (about 20 breaths), recheck the infant's pulse. If the infant still has a pulse but is not breathing, continue rescue breathing. Check the pulse every minute. Continue rescue breathing until help arrives.

SKILL SHEET

If Infant is Not Breathing...

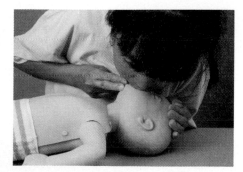

To give rescue breaths to an infant, seal your mouth over the infant's mouth and nose.

Give Rescue Breathing

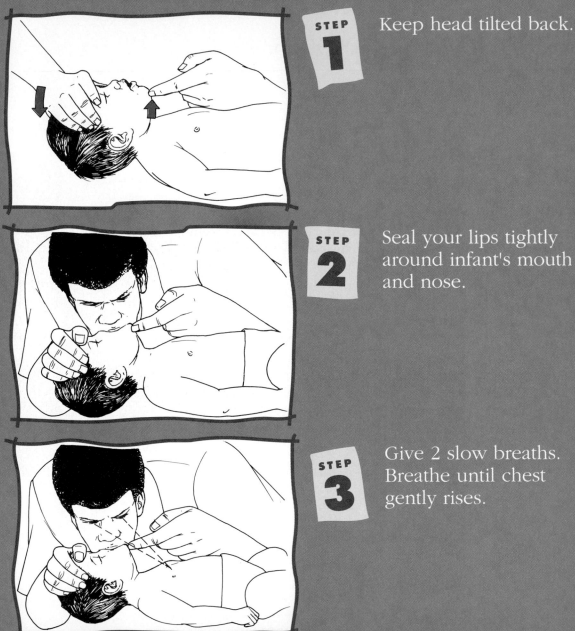

STEP 1

Keep head tilted back.

STEP 2

Seal your lips tightly around infant's mouth and nose.

STEP 3

Give 2 slow breaths. Breathe until chest gently rises.

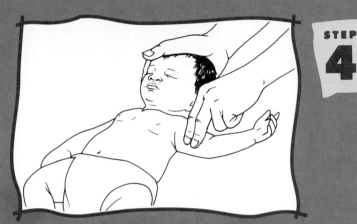

STEP 4 Check for a pulse.

If pulse is present but infant is still not breathing ...

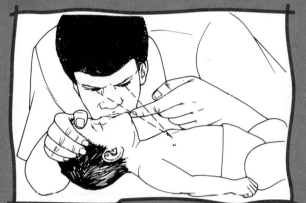

STEP 5 Give 1 slow breath about every 3 seconds. Do this for about 1 minute (20 breaths).

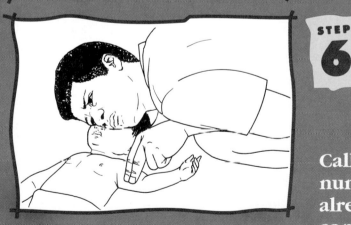

STEP 6 Recheck pulse and breathing.

Call the local emergency number if you have not already done so. Then, continue rescue breathing as long as pulse is present but infant is not breathing. Recheck pulse and breathing about every minute.

SIDS

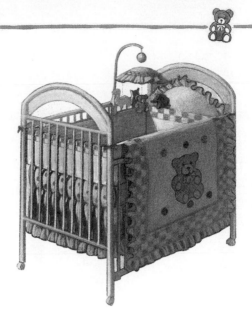

"**F**or the first few months, I would lie awake in bed at night and wonder if she was still breathing. I mean you just never know. I couldn't get to sleep until I checked on her at least once." This is how one mother described her first experience with parenting.

Sudden Infant Death Syndrome (SIDS) is the sudden, unexpected, and unexplained death of apparently healthy babies. It is the major cause of death for infants between the ages of 1 month and 1 year. In the United States, SIDS, sometimes called crib death, is responsible for the death of about 7,000 infants each year.

Because it cannot be predicted or prevented, SIDS causes many new parents to feel anxious. With no warning signs or symptoms, a sleeping infant can stop breathing and never wake again. Parents and other family members of SIDS victims often have trouble dealing with this traumatic event. Along with the stress of mourning their loss, they endure tremendous feelings of guilt, believing that they should have been able to prevent the child's death.

Researchers are working to find the cause(s) of SIDS. At this time, several risk factors—characteristics that occur more often in SIDS victims than in normal babies—have been discovered. Yet these risk factors are not causes and cannot be used to predict which infants will die. For example, 95 percent of SIDS deaths occur in infants between 2 and 4 months of age, so being in this age group is a risk factor. Other risk factors for SIDS include smoking during pregnancy, first pregnancy under 20 years of age, several children already born to the mother, a baby with a low birthweight, and a baby with a low growth rate during the mother's pregnancy.

The best prevention for SIDS, as well as many other infant diseases, is for pregnant women to practice healthy behaviors while pregnant. They should get proper prenatal care, eat a balanced diet, not smoke or drink alcholic drinks, and get adequate rest and exercise.

Some basic facts about SIDS:

- Ninety percent of SIDS deaths occur while the infant is asleep.
- SIDS deaths can occur between the ages of 2 weeks and 18 months. Ninety five percent of deaths occur between 2 and 4 months of age.
- The majority of SIDS deaths occur in fall and winter.
- Between 30 and 50 percent of SIDS victims have minor respiratory or gastrointestinal infections at the time of death.
- SIDS occurs slightly more often in boys than in girls.

For more information, call the National SIDS Resource Center at (703) 821-8955, ext. 249 or 474.

REFERENCES

National SIDS Resource Center (formerly National SIDS Clearinghouse). *Fact Sheet: SIDS Information for the EMT.* McLean, VA, 1990.

Department of Health and Human Services, Public Health Service, Health Resources and Services Administration, Maternal and Child Health Bureau. *Information Exchange: Newsletter of the National SIDS Clearinghouse.* IE32, July 1991.

If Air Won't Go In

If the infant's chest doesn't rise when you give breaths, the airway is probably blocked. It may be blocked by the infant's tongue or an object. If the infant was left alone with a bottle to drink, fluids may be blocking the airway.

You must clear the blockage immediately. First, retilt the infant's head and lift the chin. Try to give breaths again. If the breaths still don't go in, you must assume there is something blocking the airway and try to remove it. Use the same combination of back blows and chest thrusts that you used for the conscious infant.

Give 5 back blows between the shoulder blades while you hold the infant facedown on your forearm.

Then give 5 chest thrusts on the lower part of the breastbone while the infant is supported on your arm. Next, look in the infant's mouth for the object. If you can see it, remove it with your finger. Then give 2 breaths to try to get oxygen into the infant's lungs. Continue the back blows, chest thrusts, and breaths until the infant coughs the object up or begins to breathe or cough.

*I*f you are unable to breathe into an infant, the airway is probably blocked. Give 5 back blows and 5 chest thrusts.

SKILL SHEET

If Air Does Not Go In...

Give Back Blows and Chest Thrusts

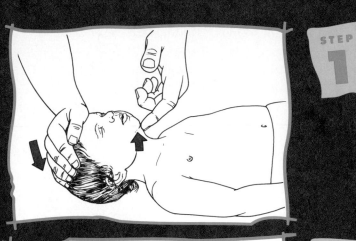

STEP 1 Retilt infant's head.

STEP 2 Give breaths again.

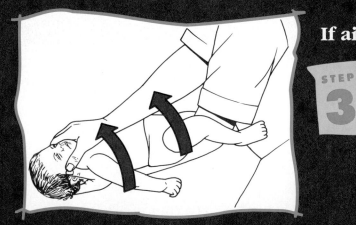

If air still won't go in ...

STEP 3 Position infant face-down on forearm.

STEP 4

Give 5 back blows with heel of hand between infant's shoulder blades.

STEP 5

Position infant faceup on forearm.

continued ▸

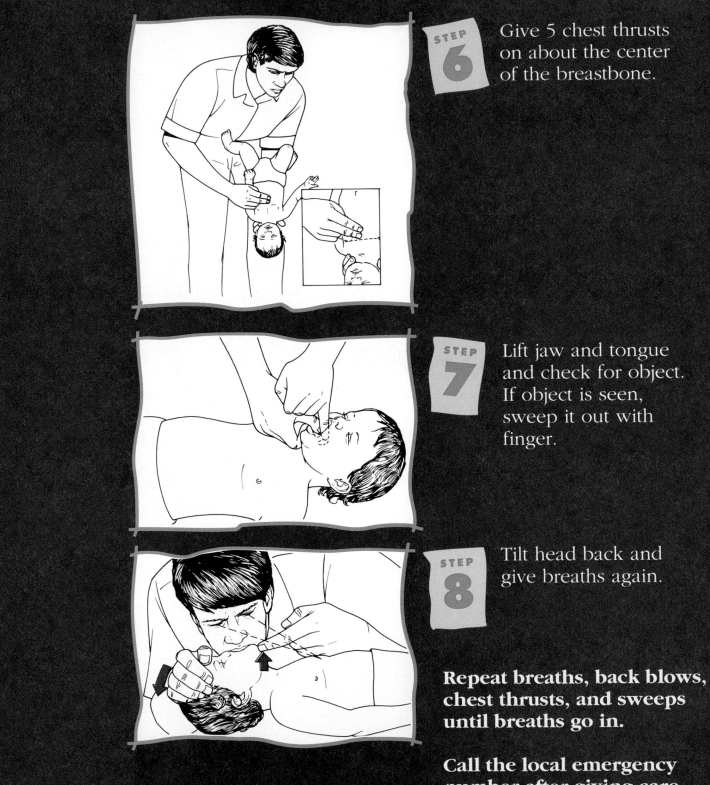

STEP 6 Give 5 chest thrusts on about the center of the breastbone.

STEP 7 Lift jaw and tongue and check for object. If object is seen, sweep it out with finger.

STEP 8 Tilt head back and give breaths again.

Repeat breaths, back blows, chest thrusts, and sweeps until breaths go in.

Call the local emergency number after giving care for 1 minute if you have not already done so.

If an Infant Does Not Have a Pulse

An infant who is not breathing and does not have a pulse needs CPR. Feel for an infant's pulse on the inside of the upper arm, between the infant's elbow and shoulder. Start CPR if you can't feel the pulse after checking for about 5 seconds.

To give CPR, place the infant on his or her back on a hard surface, such as the floor or a table. If you have to move the infant to the telephone so you can call for help, the hard surface can be your hand or forearm, with your palm supporting the infant's back. Place two fingers on the breastbone just below an imaginary line between the nipples and give 5 compressions. These should take about 3 seconds. Count "one, two, three, four, five, . . ." to help keep a regular and even rhythm.

After giving five compressions, give 1 slow breath (about 1½ seconds). Then begin compressions again. Do 12 cycles of 5 compressions and 1 breath (about 1 minute). Then recheck the pulse. If you can't feel the pulse, continue with cycles of 5 compressions and 1 breath until help arrives. Check every few minutes for pulse and breathing.

Ask someone to call the local emergency number as soon as you find out that the infant is unconscious. If you are alone, give CPR for about 1 minute, then make the call yourself. If you can, carry the infant to the telephone so that you can continue giving CPR.

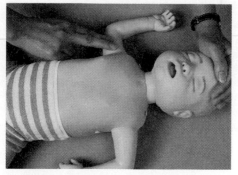

Feel for an infant's pulse on the inside of the upper arm, between the infant's elbow and shoulder.

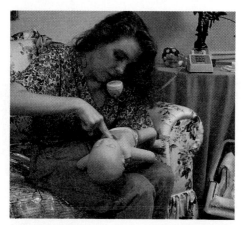

The hard surface of your hand or forearm can be used to support an infant during CPR if you have to move to a phone.

If Infant is Not Breathing and Has No Pulse...

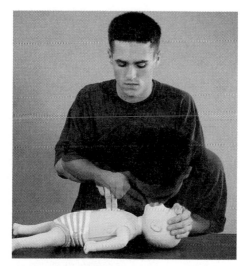

An infant who is not breathing and does not have a pulse needs CPR. Alternate giving five chest compressions and one breath.

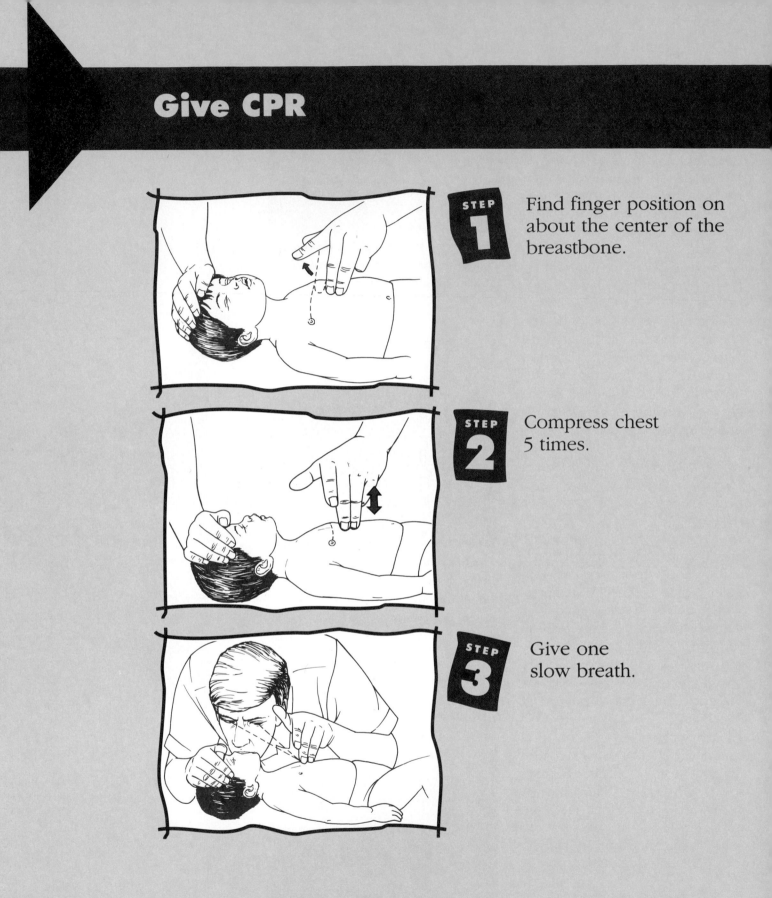

STEP 1 Find finger position on about the center of the breastbone.

STEP 2 Compress chest 5 times.

STEP 3 Give one slow breath.

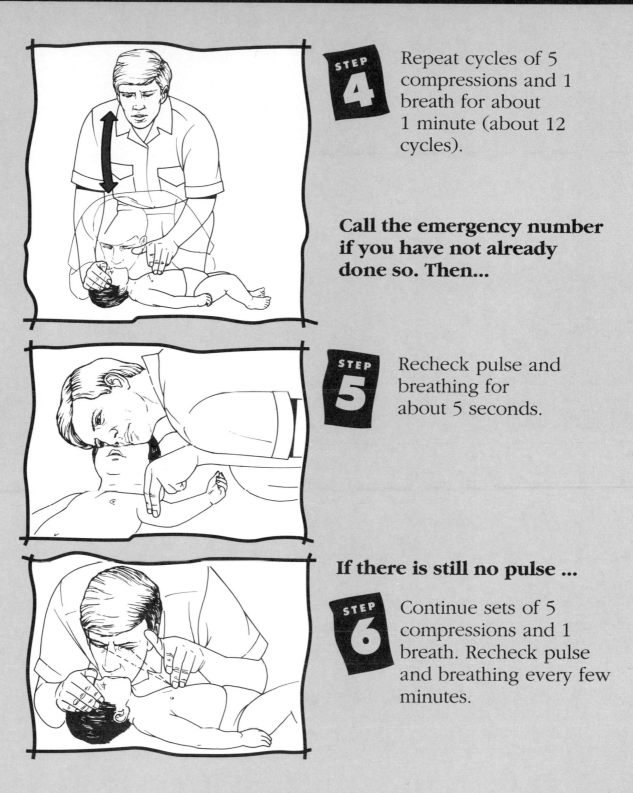

STEP 4

Repeat cycles of 5 compressions and 1 breath for about 1 minute (about 12 cycles).

Call the emergency number if you have not already done so. Then...

STEP 5

Recheck pulse and breathing for about 5 seconds.

If there is still no pulse ...

STEP 6

Continue sets of 5 compressions and 1 breath. Recheck pulse and breathing every few minutes.

INDEX

Shock to restore heart rhythm, 64-65
SIDS, 114
Smoking and heart disease, 72, 73
Stoma, rescue breathing for person with, 50
Stomach of child, avoiding getting air into, 94-95
Stress and healthy life-style, 35
Stroke, 70
Sudden Infant Death Syndrome, 114
Supplies for first aid kit, 22

T

Thrusts
  abdominal, 44-46
    on child, 91-92, 98-101

Thrusts—cont'd
  abdominal—cont'd
    with rescue breathing, 51-55
  chest, for infants, 116-118
TIA, 70
Transient ischemic attack, 70

U

Unconscious child, rescue breathing for, 94
Unconscious victim, checking, 30-31, 32-33

V

Ventricular fibrillation, 64-65
Victim
  checking, 28-34

Victim—cont'd
  conscious, checking, 31, 34
  moving, 15, 16-17
  unconscious, checking, 30-31, 32-33
Virus, human immunodeficiency, transmission of, 7
Vomiting
  and breathing emergency, 38
  in child, 94, 95
  during rescue breathing, 50

W

Weight and heart disease, 75

NOTES

NOTES

NOTES